T0146519

This
Energy Healing Stuff
Is
For Real

Susan Olencki Giangiulio

BALBOA.
PRESS

A DIVISION OF HAY HOUSE

Balboa Press books may be ordered through booksellers or by contacting:

Balboa Press
A Division of Hay House
1663 Liberty Drive
Bloomington, IN 47403
www.balboapress.com
1 (877) 407-4847

Because of the dynamic nature of the Internet, any web addresses or links contained in this book may have changed since publication and may no longer be valid. The views expressed in this work are solely those of the author and do not necessarily reflect the views of the publisher, and the publisher hereby disclaims any responsibility for them.

The author of this book does not dispense medical advice or prescribe the use of any technique as a form of treatment for physical, emotional, or medical problems without the advice of a physician, either directly or indirectly. The intent of the author is only to offer information of a general nature to help you in your quest for emotional and spiritual well-being. In the event you use any of the information in this book for yourself, which is your constitutional right, the author and the publisher assume no responsibility for your actions.

Any people depicted in stock imagery provided by Getty Images are models, and such images are being used for illustrative purposes only. Certain stock imagery © Getty Images.

Print information available on the last page.

ISBN: 978-1-9822-2687-9 (sc)
ISBN: 978-1-9822-2686-2 (hc)
ISBN: 978-1-9822-2699-2 (e)

Library of Congress Control Number: 2019904928

Balboa Press rev. date: 05/08/2019

What people are saying about *Emotional Healing...*

I have been around the field of science and medicine for quite some time - long enough to know from even the most basic chemistry that every particle, atom, and structure has an energy, vibration and frequency. People and animals are not excluded from that. We also know that things don't have to physically touch to interact. Non-physical energy healing is something that was in my awareness, but it has always been something that I never fully understood or have ever utilized. However, when I found myself on the verge of losing my dog, Pistol, because his fear and anxiety had gotten him in serious trouble, I was given the opportunity to try energy healing with him. Pistol was not physically present in the room during the session; however, by the next time I saw Pistol, he was a different dog. He had a history of prior abuse and neglect and was easily frightened, anxious, always on high alert, and often unpredictable. After the healing work was done, he was noticeably calmer and had a much more even keel. I experienced a similar change in myself when I had energy work done on me. I felt the anxiety and stress ease almost completely during the session. I could feel my posture change and tension release from my neck and back. Every emotion that was released was spot on with events from my past and my current life, and they were emotions that I had suppressed. It was truly incredible to experience the release and healing. *Gabriel W., DC*

* * * * *

I was about to turn 40, and – from the outside – my life looked pretty good. I had a great job, beautiful house, wonderful husband, family, and friends. But, on the inside I was unhappy, vacant, exhausted, and depressed. I was so tired of trying to give the appearance that everything was OK, and it was taking its toll on me. I wanted to enjoy this journey of life but realized my baggage was over the weight limit and something needed to be done. This eventually led me to energy healing, specifically emotional release healing. There was something about these healing techniques that made sense to me – how everything that connected positively, negatively, physically, emotionally, subconsciously, and unconsciously affected my whole being. This was definitely something worth checking out because what I was doing wasn't working, and I needed to get better.

Emotional release healing has helped me deal with painful events from my past and identified what was causing the emotional and physical issues in the present. Working with specific emotional release techniques helped me understand why I was feeling the way I was, clarified what I was experiencing and taught me how to manage, understand, and effectively release trapped emotions caused by the traumatic events in my life. I have gone all the way back to my past lives, to inception, to birth, to different age groups in my lifetime, and to the present in order to heal and release the trapped emotions caused by the events during those times. It gave each event a voice, each feeling worth, and most importantly gave me a voice to speak my truth.

I am so grateful and have grown so much from where I started in this journey of recovery, self-acceptance, forgiveness, and love. I am so appreciative of emotional release healing because it has empowered me with the tools and strategies to continue to heal subconsciously, consciously, and physically so that I can enjoy every experience in my life adventure. *China F., artist*

* * * * *

I honestly feel emotional release therapy saved my life. After eight years of traditional therapy, I really did not see or feel any improvement. It was a small step forward, three back. Emotional release has not only improved my life in a few sessions, but it has also helped restore me to who I am as a person. I am so very grateful for having found emotional release healing. *Kimberly D., small business owner*

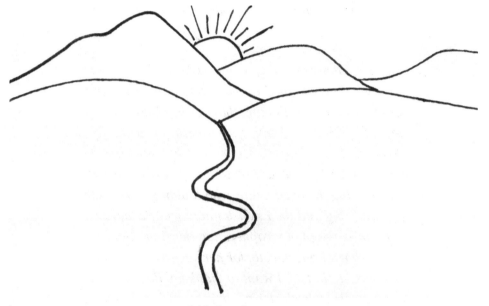

Life is a journey...

This book is dedicated to everyone I have ever known who has been a part of my becoming who I am today. In particular, I want to mention my deceased friend and mentor, Jeannie Gay, who "awakened" me to trusting God/Universe.

I am also full of gratitude for, and wish to acknowledge, those who have helped to make this book a reality: Leanna Conley, for lighting that literary flame within me; Ashley Hall, for helping me with the basic outline, after which my fingers became all but attached to the computer keyboard; Linda W., my always upbeat, encouraging, beloved editor who taught me so much about writing and the English language; Barbara G. and Janie, my photographers for the final chapter; and Barbara Robertaccio, for her keen eye for detail. And most definitely, I want to thank my Barbara (my twin), my trustworthy friend Sharon, and my husband Tony for their steadfast encouragement and their belief in me.

A heart-to-heart hug to you all!

This energy healing stuff is for real....

Over the time frame of a few years, I studied several energy healing modalities. I was curious enough to take some classes but wasn't totally convinced they were effective. While studying one modality, a class facilitator told me I analyzed everything too much! Well, of course I did. I still trusted my doctors because they were *medical* people. This energy stuff was something I had not been raised to believe in, yet I was beginning to open up....sort of.

I was on the fence.

In time, I experienced what I consider to be a profound healing experience with a woman at a metaphysical fair. She used her voice as a healing modality. *Hhmmm.* There just might be something to this energy healing stuff after all.

Then, one day, I contacted a medical intuit I had briefly seen (as in seen at a table selling her wares at a training event). She lived in Arizona, and I lived in Florida, so we spoke on the phone. I asked her if she could heal my injured tailbone. The discomfort was constant, sometimes intense. Medical doctors had told me there was little to be done, if anything, for an injured tailbone; however, the medical intuit said she'd be happy to work on it. Could she really heal this broken set of bones? Sure enough, as we talked, I *felt* the bones move into position! Since that moment, I have had no tailbone discomfort whatsoever. None.

Soon afterward, I jumped off the fence. I have been an energy healing advocate ever since.

Table of Contents

Prelude

The mind is everything; what you think you become.

~ **Socrates**

One afternoon, a friend invited me to her son's birthday party. When I walked in, I quickly realized I knew no one else at the party. However, one woman greeted me as if we had been friends for years. I had no clue who she was, but it certainly was a pleasant welcome to the party. I meandered through the throng of guests to introduce myself, and we began a wonderful, fruitful conversation.

Leanna and I had a lot in common. We both were from the Detroit area of Michigan. We both had attended the University of Michigan. We both had lived in California and in New York City. Leanna had many dear friends who had been enrolled in U-M's Art Department, which was housed in the same building as the School of Architecture and Design where my father was a professor. His name even sounded familiar to her. *Kool.*

Leanna was sort of a jill-of-all-trades. She had multiple talents and could claim numerous accomplishments, which included being both an artist and a published author. When she inquired about what I did, I told her about emotional release healing, a form of energy healing. She was genuinely interested and asked me all sorts of questions. Keeping HIPAA (Health Insurance Portability & Accountability Act - 1996) in mind, I shared with her the results of a few healing sessions. After a few stories, she exclaimed that I ought to write a book about what I do. So here is the book, the result of that one chance meeting. *Gratitude.*

I have written this book because I would like you, the reader, to realize the importance of several concepts: a) living with *gratitude,* b) living with faith, c) living with intention, and d) understanding the power of unresolved emotions and how they affect the body. Although this book will dabble in the scientific aspects of the spirit, body, and mind connection, it will concentrate on examples of everyday life experiences and how having gratitude and faith, living with intention, and processing emotions can shift one's thinking. AND how, when one's thinking changes, one's health and outlook on life will also change. I hope to explain the concepts in everyday language so that scientific or medical jargon does not get in the way of comprehending what I wish to share.

Plenty of folks have written books about how they have cured themselves – through a certain way of thinking, a certain lifestyle, or a certain diet – of "incurable" dis-eases. This is not such a book, nor is it about the latest, the greatest, or the newest healing modality, or method. Dis-ease means a lack of ease within the body whereas disease tends to mean an illness or a lack of health. This book is about the pursuit of ease within the body and mind.

I have and have had a relatively typical life and will share much of it in this book to show how I have shifted my way of thinking, and my diet, to improve my general health. Even with the many challenges life presents, I am now much better able to handle them. If I can make such a shift, I believe you can, too. Much of the book is filled with stories about my experiences, or those of my clients, and the rest of the book is written as a guide to those who are "awakening" to the wonders of energy healing and emotional healing.

Gratitude is expressing thanksgiving and appreciation for all blessings in life, both large and small. Gratitude allows you to maintain optimism even in the presence of negativity and to see the positive in everything, even if it is miniscule. Living in gratitude allows you to become the proactive activator in your life, minimizing the woe-is-me mindset. Express gratitude when, as you drive, all the traffic lights are green; express gratitude when you find a spot in a crowded parking lot; express gratitude when someone unexpectedly holds a door open for you; express gratitude when the sun is shining, and, yes, even when it is raining. Get the idea? The more you express gratitude, the more open you are to abundance. The more you express gratitude, the more you can live in the moment and the more able you are to process emotions. And the fewer emotions that get stuck, the better your life will flow, and the more content, more compassionate, and less judgmental you will become. When you live in gratitude, and with gratitude, your life and health improve. You'll find that when you say "thank you" it comes heartfelt. The power of gratitude and self-love is not to be underestimated. It is powerful.

Living with faith allows one to trust there is more than just the here and now, that we are part of a larger plan for life.

Living with intention is living with a goal or purpose in mind. Even the simple task of creating a daily to-do list is an act of setting an intention. Whatever form it takes, living with intention is a driving force – from deep within – that moves you forward.

Trapped emotions, I believe, are at the root of dis-ease and its countless symptoms. They are one of the greatest obstacles to your well-being and health. An emotion is an e-motion, or energy in motion. It's a vibration. A trapped emotion is the energy of emotion that did not/could not get processed by the subconscious and, therefore, literally got stuck someplace in the body. This will be discussed throughout the book.

* * * * *

I begin this book about energy healing with the premise that we are all spiritual beings living a human experience. Have you ever thought about what that actually means? As spiritual beings, we are all energy beings. As spiritual beings, we are all love. Anything that is incongruent with love will eventually manifest as a symptom.

At first, many considered energy healing hokey, a form of quackery. However, as more and more people "awaken" to this way of thinking, it is becoming a common practice. It is how I have chosen to live, and to heal myself, on a daily basis. Granted, a few times this body required surgery to heal properly, yet I was able to add emotional healing and energy healing to speed up the recovery process. It also has kept me out of the "why me?!" and "woe-is-me" negative mindset, thus keeping me focused on gratitude and healing.

I use the terms "emotional healing" and "energy healing" interchangeably in this book. My opinion is that emotional healing removes the negative, stuck emotions from the body and is a subset of energy healing.

The more I live in gratitude, the more I live in faith, the more I set intentions, and the more I practice emotional healing, the more I connect to the Infinite Abundance of God/Universe. And so can you...

1. Everything Is Energy

For one who believes, no proof is necessary. For the nonbeliever, no amount of proof is sufficient.

~ Saint Ignatius of Loyola

Energy healing can be powerful, and the following story astounds even me with how powerful that can be. Years ago at a party, I met an extended family new to our community. The family had moved into the area that October, in hopes of a better future, but, so far, their landlord, an unpleasant human being [and I'm being extremely polite here], had made the move very challenging. Generally uncooperative, he kept lying to them, especially by making empty promises about much needed yard maintenance and house repairs.

The young mother was pregnant with her second child. When I heard Baby Zoe was due the first week of December, I blurted out that she would be a Thanksgiving-week baby instead. A couple of weeks later, I learned Baby Zoe had turned breech. The grandmother, a nurse, knew the challenges of a breech birth and, because we had discussed energy healing, approached me to see if I could help. Through muscle testing, I was able to ask Baby Zoe if it was her intention to be born breech. Despite the fact she had been absorbing some of her mother's negative emotions, her response was "No." Over the next few days, I released a few emotions from the grandmother, the mother, and the baby.

Within the week, Baby Zoe righted herself and got into the birth canal. The grandmother was ecstatic. Then, the number "27" kept flashing in my mind. *Incessantly.* So I called both the mother and grandmother a few days before Thanksgiving and told them I was putting my reputation on the line, for I then stated the baby would be born on the 27th. The grandmother called me on the 28th to let me know Baby Zoe had indeed been born on November 27th at 5:01 in the morning!

After they brought the baby home, I visited the family and held her. Although a newborn, she looked straight at me with wide-open eyes. Her mother and grandmother were amazed. She had not looked at either of them in that way. We all sensed, simultaneously, that Baby Zoe intuitively knew who I was. What a gift she gave me! She was saying thank you.

How could this be? How could I energetically *unbreech* Baby Zoe? How did I *know* she would be born earlier than expected? And how did I *know* that date would be November 27th?

The answer is simple. EVERYTHING is energy.

* * * * *

Different terminologies can be used to define energy, and it depends on whether one is speaking scientifically or metaphysically, and on whether one is speaking from a Western or an Eastern perspective. For the purpose of this book, I will use the Eastern, metaphysical definition and will define energy as the body's life force.

Following are just a few of the terms used to describe energy:

a. *Chi/Qi/Ki* – The ancient Chinese, as far back as the 3rd millennium B.C., claimed the existence of a vital energy, composed of two polar forces, yin and yang. When both forces are balanced, the body and the mind are balanced. "Ki" is the Japanese term for the living energy that connects us all.

b. *Aura* – An aura is an "invisible," ever changing flow of life energy around one's body or around an object. It is any "invisible" emanation or subtle light surrounding someone or something. I placed quotes around "invisible" because some people claim to *see* auras, and there are special cameras that photograph them. Also, auras have colors, similar to how chakras have colors. The colors have meaning and can tell about a person's state of being and health.

c. *Prana* – The Indian culture uses this term for universal energy. Prana is considered the breath of life that moves through all forms and gives life to everything.

d. The list goes on....

Everything in the universe is made up of atoms; therefore, so are our bodies. Because atoms are interacting fields of energy, we are all energy. As Albert Einstein illustrated with his famous equation, $E=mc^2$, "Mass is Energy and Energy is Mass." It should not be surprising, then, that Einstein encouraged the advent of energy healing. After all, he had proven scientifically that the body, as well as all of life, is energy, and all energy is interrelated.

So, if everything is energy, then we are energy. Therefore, we are all connected. Let me give you some additional examples:

- Have you ever gone into a room or a house and felt your surroundings were a bit creepy? You sensed the negative energy in the environment.

- Have you ever met someone and, for some "unknown" reason, found yourself turned off by the person? It may have been because your energy was of a higher or lower vibration than the other person.

- In contrast, have you ever met someone and been attracted to the person right away, again, for some "unknown" reason? It may have been the person's vibration matched your vibration.

- Have you ever had company stay with you for a day or two (or longer) and then sense an emptiness shortly after they have left, even if you were grateful to have your space back? This void, this emptiness within your home, is because the energy of your guest(s) is no longer there.

Consciously or subconsciously, we are all attuned to various vibrations or energies, whether they are positive or negative. We are all connected. We are all spiritual beings, and as such, we are all energy (with our own vibrations) – and pure love. If you are like me, when I was first introduced to energy healing, you may think energy work is weird, wacky, you name it. I'd like to reassure the neophyte. Eventually, it will all make sense.

Each emotion, word, thought, sound, memory and so forth has its own vibration. Some of these are low vibration and negative. Some are high vibration and positive. Negative vibrations attract other negative vibrations while higher vibrations attract other higher vibrations. Have you ever noticed how, once you start thinking a negative thought, your mind goes off on a tangent and, before you realize it, you've created a whole negative scenario in your mind? Has your negative thinking ever gone so far that your heart starts to race or you find yourself in a bad mood? The creation of negative mental scenarios, with or without the racing heart and bad mood, are examples of negative vibrations attracting negative vibrations.

At the other end of the spectrum, as you think or feel positive thoughts, your mood tends to improve, and the world around you seems to improve. The more positively you perceive life, the more often positive experiences present themselves to you. A positive intention is high vibrational energy. Positive or high vibrations attract other positive or high vibrations. A healthy body has a higher vibration than a body that is out of balance or ill. To take this even further, processed food is of a low vibration; fresh food is of a high vibration. Considering the positive nature of high vibrations, why would anyone eat something of low vibrations?

The old adage "Sticks and stones may break my bones, but words will never hurt me" is so false. Remember, words are energy. Therefore, a negative word, with its negative vibration, *can* be emotionally hurtful. Think of those who are verbally or emotionally abused. What state of being are they in? Some sort of façade of happiness? An obviously sad state? An insecure state? Do they seem to be inundated with feelings of unworthiness? Oh, negative words do hurt. And they do so because they produce negative energy.

Dr. Masaru Emoto, in his many books on water, clearly demonstrated how music, words, and even thoughts affect water molecules.[1] Although the actual amount is debatable, our bodies are roughly 60% water (with infants averaging between 70-75% water).[2] Imagine, therefore, the impact music, words, and thoughts have on our bodies, especially on the bodies of infants. We are very much affected, whether or not we are aware of it.

During his experiments, Dr. Emoto took photos of water crystals using a special camera. The crystals exposed to heavy metal music became masses of unappealing matter. They were *not* beautiful. What *was* beautiful were the crystals exposed to relaxing contemporary or classical music. Similar results occurred when Dr. Emoto compared crystals exposed to hateful words versus loving words, as well as hateful thoughts versus loving thoughts. Again, remember, everything is energy.

If we accept the concept that words, thoughts, and sounds do affect our being, we must consider how fetuses and very young babies can be affected by each of them. Remember the negative emotions in the household while Baby Zoe was *in utero*? Far too often parents fail to realize little children are like sponges, taking in everything from their surroundings. In fact, the most significant development of the brain occurs by the age of three. If a fetus is unwanted or unloved, it will sense it. If a child is abused or neglected, and if they are unable to verbalize or to process their emotions, as they become older, these unresolved issues could manifest as unacceptable behaviors or as physical or emotional symptoms.

Doc Childre and his coauthors explain in *The Heartmath Solution* that the heart is formed before the brain. When the brain does form, the development begins at the base of the brain stem and moves up into the emotional centers of the brain. They write, "In an unborn child there's an emotional brain long before there's a rational one, and a beating heart before either." [3] No wonder fetuses in the early stages of development are able to absorb trapped emotions from the mother! Imagine…. What would happen if pregnant women could have emotional release healing before giving birth? Just think about how much less anger and frustration there would be in the world if babies came into this world with only love and positive energy. One could argue that coming into the world with subconscious unprocessed emotional "baggage" could be part of the life path of a soon-to-be-born child. However, I dream of babies entering this world free of emotional baggage.

Energy not only connects us, it is in a constant state of being exchanged. Have you ever thought about a living person you know, and, before long, they've called you, sent you a message, or run into you while you were out and about? This happens because we are all energy. And, in such cases, the people you are thinking about are energetically picking up on the vibrations created by your thoughts. However long it takes, it happens because your energy is communicating with theirs.

* * * * *

SUSAN OLENCKI GIANGIULIO

Traditional Chinese medicine suggests dis-ease occurs when the channels used for energy exchange are blocked in some way. As long ago as 5,000 years ago, the Chinese discovered certain emotions tend to originate or get stuck in certain organs or meridians. For example, anger and its associated emotions tend to originate and to get stuck in the liver/gall bladder meridians. (While some talk about happy drunks, they ought to really ask about why people get inebriated in the first place. Many do so to mask emotions such as anger, depression, and frustration.) In a similar manner, grief and its associated emotions tend to get stuck in the lungs/small intestines meridians, and fear tends to get stuck in the bladder/kidneys meridians.

The fascinating thing is that, if an organ is removed, the energy of that organ may still remain. *Yes, indeedy.* I had a client who had her gall bladder removed years ago. Nevertheless, while doing emotional release healing with her, that organ came up multiple times. Apparently, even though her gall bladder was gone, the energy trapped by that organ was still around. What a concept. The question is whether or not she might still have her gall bladder if she had done intensive emotional release prior to surgery.

If emotions are energy, which cannot remain static, then energy represents movement and change. And change is the essence of life. Even if you feel as if your life is stagnant, and as routine as the sunrise and sunset, realize that each sunrise and sunset is unique and welcomes a new and different day or night. And, as the days turn into weeks, the seasons inevitably come and go. Life is in constant motion.

In your high school science class, you learned about atoms and their electrons, protons, and neutrons. You learned that all these subatomic particles help produce energy because they are always in motion. In fact, energy must move, or disruptions will occur.

So, what happens when the flow of energy is disrupted or stopped? For a down-to-earth example of stopped up energy, all we have to do is imagine what happens when a toilet gets stopped up. In this case, the energy of flowing water literally stops flowing. And the result is a mess. Another example is when a transformer blows out on an electric pole. Because the electric energy no longer flows, there is a loss of electric power for those in the vicinity, a loss which can last from hours to days, or even weeks.

Simply stated, then, unprocessed or blocked energy reacts in a similar way within our bodies. When it's not flowing, it gets stuck and causes disruptions. The disruptions can, for example, manifest as having the blahs, feeling sad, or having depressed energy. They can also appear as physical symptoms such as pain, discomfort, or dis-ease. Such imbalances are your body's way of telling you it is out of balance – that you are out of balance – and the resulting disruptions are a cry for help from your body.

2. Trapped Emotions

I'm always very aware of all that I've been through. I wanted to box it up, but that doesn't work long-term.

~ **Michelle Stevens**, *People Magazine*, **March 27, 2017**

So, how do trapped emotions occur?

Energy imbalances, due to trapped emotions, can occur in multiple ways, even to children and animals. Trapped emotions can be inherited or absorbed. They can develop because a person does not live in the moment. They can also occur when a person becomes overly stressed, even by just dealing with daily life. Following are examples of each.

Inherited Emotions

If one stops to think about it, we are the creation of both of our parents. We not only inherit DNA from both sides of our parents' families, we also inherit their trapped emotions, held in cellular memory, sometimes through multiple generations.

> *Nancy, a friend, had a weak left arm. One day we were just visiting. When I learned her left arm had always been weak, I asked if I could do some emotional release work with her. She agreed but was not sure what she should expect. A few released emotions later, after a miasm, or a maladaptive inherited energy came up, she revealed her Dad had suffered the effects of polio on his left side. She then understood the emotional*

connection she had to her father's dis-ease. The next day, her left arm was "normal."

Absorbed Emotions

Trapped emotions can occur by subconsciously absorbing them from others. By the way, this is particularly true for empaths, those who sense other's emotions, especially if they forget to protect their own energy fields.

> *One time I was in an office waiting to speak with someone who was finishing other business. A man I knew came into the office. When we began chatting to pass the time, I was feeling fine. However, as he shared information about his daughter's upcoming surgery, I felt as if I had just been gut punched. The pain was intense, and I felt like I was going to either pass out or puke. I left without talking to the person I went to see. When I got into my car, I did emotional release on myself. Because my emotions seemed inappropriate for the situation, I asked my higher self if these emotions belonged to me. The answer was "No." To whom did they belong? They belonged to the man I was chatting with in the office. Why was I feeling them? As an empath, I had not put up my protective energetic shield, and I had absorbed his emotions. I took a few moments to clear the emotions, and I energetically sent them into the loving white light of God. I kid you not, as soon as I did all this, the gut-punched feeling disappeared. Completely.*

* * *

> *I worked with a baby who cried for a good week after being born. By a fluke, the parents discovered*

the baby's collarbone had been broken during birth. With the mother's permission, I released several emotions, including a few (such as "guilt") the infant had absorbed from the nurse who had assisted in the birthing process. What struck me was that the trapped emotions could have easily affected the rest of this baby's life and given him challenges into adulthood.

* * *

A male client often spoke with a teenager in his extended family. Due to her parents' divorce, she was experiencing major trauma in her life. We discovered that the majority of the emotions released during our sessions had to do with the client absorbing the emotions of his teenaged relative.

Absorbed Emotions *in Utero*

As an energy healing practitioner, I am finding that emotions absorbed *in utero* play a major factor in many people's lives. During any state of development, the fetus absorbs emotions primarily from the mother in the womb. These emotions are not inherited as they did not arrive with the parents' sperm and egg.

Baby Zoe is an example of absorbed emotions *in utero.* Her emotions were absorbed by her as a soon-to-be-born baby. If I had been unable to help release the emotions she had absorbed from her mother, she would have grown up with those emotions and not been aware of where they came from or why she had them. The resulting symptoms would have been almost impossible to trace.

I am an example of having absorbed my mother's emotions when she learned she was having twins. I was unaware of these emotions until I was a full-grown adult. Through emotional release work, I now realize some of the physical challenges I face are a direct result of those trapped emotions *in utero.*

> *A mother had privately wondered if her 10-year-old son was on the autism spectrum. She wondered if there were any trapped emotions manifesting as his behavior issues, and asked if I would work with her son. I agreed. She was present the entire time in case either her son or I had any questions. Every single one of his emotions (and there were at least 10 of them in this spontaneous session) was an absorbed emotion from his time* in utero. *When I questioned the mother, she shared that she did experience many emotionally stressful situations while she was pregnant. The mother continued to work on the issues that came up in our session, and I am happy to report that she, and her son, have both noticed a shift in his demeanor and behavior.*

Not-In-the-Moment Living

A very common way to develop trapped emotions or energetic imbalances is not being focused, not being in the moment, not being mindful. Put another way, we can trap emotions when we live by habit or when we are not paying attention to our actions and emotions.

How often do you misplace your keys or some other item you use every day? How many times have you driven from Point A to Point B and not remembered how you did it, particularly if it is a route you drive all the time? Such questions help point out everyday examples of not-in-the-moment living.

> *A client shared with me how her husband functions out of habit every workday morning. When he gets up, he uses an old-fashioned, individual serving*

coffeepot to make his coffee, from scratch, on the stove. The problem is one interruption can completely offset his routine. For example, he has, on several occasions, forgotten to put water in the base of the coffee pot, causing it to overheat...a lot. A person who lives mechanically, out of habit, often has to deal with such circumstances – circumstances that can affect, even harm, their possessions, their bodies, and their relationships.

When people live by habit, they react rather than make choices. And because they are not "in the moment," they are seldom aware of their actions. However, it makes life so much easier to process if you are aware of your thoughts and movements. This is not to be confused with calculated or manipulative actions; this has more to do with actions coming from a focused inner peace and calm knowingness.

On Overload

One of the easiest ways to create an energetic imbalance, or a trapped emotion, is to live on overload – that is, to become overly stressed, in either a negative or positive direction. Indeed, stress is one of the prime culprits in creating energetic imbalances within the body.

When on overload, you cannot properly process the emotions, thoughts, or events you need to deal with each day. In order to cope, you stuff the emotions away, consciously or subconsciously, and your emotions get blocked. Examples of being on overload include such negative things as being in or witnessing a disaster, getting fired, being involved in an accident, hearing traumatic news, dealing with injury or disease, moving (which can be a negative or a positive event), or filing for divorce. Stress overload, though, can also occur with positive events: taking on a new job, planning a wedding, or preparing for a competition or performance.

One of my personal stories of overload occurred during the 1989 Loma Prieta earthquake in San Francisco. I was alone in an elevator, nearing the end of the workday, when the 6.9 earthquake struck. The ensuing events left me in shock and fear, yet I felt strangely excited by the adventure. I kept my composure – because I needed to – until days later when I was out of San Francisco and safe in Sacramento, where my twin, and my boyfriend at the time, lived. A day or so afterward, at church, I totally lost it and broke down into uncontrollable tears. I cried because of an immense gratitude for not being physically harmed. During and after the earthquake, I had experienced too many emotions, sights, sounds, and smells to process, so, subconsciously, I stuffed it all away in the guise of embracing an adventure and wanting to appear emotionally strong. When I lost it in church, my tears released only the emotions trapped on the surface. It took years for me to overcome the trauma of it all.

* * *

Several years ago, I worked with a client solely on the phone. Because she lived in another city about two hours away, we never met in person but scheduled one session per week for eight weeks. Each time we spoke, she mentioned how much better she felt. The vast majority of her trapped emotions had occurred two years prior, when her mother died. The death was too much for the woman to bear, and she all but shut down. Because the emotions were so intense, she was unable to process them and her body presented with symptoms which the doctors were seemingly unable to address. Eventually, we met when I gave a presentation in the city where she lived. A woman spoke, and I immediately recognized the voice. It was this client. As she looked at me, the very first words out of her mouth were "You saved my life." Wow! I asked if she would give a testimonial. She obliged. She looked at me as she addressed the group and again used the exact same words: "You saved my life." What a testimonial! She admitted there was still work to be done, but, for the moment, she was fine. And alive.

Daily Life

Energy imbalances or trapped emotions can occur at any time as we are out and about living life: sitting in traffic jams, having dental work done, being stressed at work, living through childhood traumas, recovering from surgery, overcoming birthing challenges, moving, getting a divorce – basically, any situation perceived primarily as negative. Even seemingly insignificant events – such as someone not calling when they said they would or someone not showing up to an event you really wanted them to attend – can create trapped emotions. And sometimes we may feel it is "safer" not to express a negative emotion. As a result, that emotion gets repressed, stuffed, and ultimately stuck.

Babies and young children can develop trapped emotions due to their inability to express their emotions effectively. If babies experience trauma at a very early age, they do not have the words to express themselves, so they cry, and cry a lot, and cry intensely. Then, when they get a little older, their emotions become trapped because they often cannot express themselves without getting reprimanded.

A local public speaker came to me to help her become a relaxed public speaker. She had great trepidation about public speaking even though this is what she did in her business. We released a few emotions. As we got to one of the emotions, she let out a cry that sounded as if it came from a baby. Afterwards, she explained that all these years she had been trying to please her father. The cry was about her being a two-year-old child re-experiencing the emotion we had just released. Once we were done, she felt much lighter. When I saw her a few months later, she informed me that public speaking was no longer scary. It had actually become enjoyable.

* * *

During an emotional release healing session with Oscar, I released multiple emotions through the process of muscle testing. Keep in mind, that in the work I do, I do not encourage shrink-type discussions in my sessions. I've found the less I know, the more effective the session seems to be because whatever comes to my mind (or is downloaded, as I say), is pure energy. It does not come from my ego brain. I ask the client for just enough information for me to enable the client to see the forest as well as the trees. In Oscar's case, the story that unfolded through the released emotions had to do with the age of five. So, when all the emotions were released for that particular session, I asked Oscar what significance age five could have had in his life. It turned out his father had left the family when Oscar was five years old. When Oscar realized what he had just learned, the deep furrow on his brow relaxed.

Dr. Darren R. Weissman, author of *The Power of Infinite Love & Gratitude*, says that "Recurrent symptoms and chronic stress are the warning signs that emotions are trapped within the subconscious mind." [4] He goes on to say that energy imbalances or trapped emotions all begin with a denied, disconnected, internalized, broken, or lost emotion within the subconscious mind. Initially, I like to explain this to my clients by saying the emotion was "smooshed", unable to come to fruition, or was never processed.

Remember, we are energy, and all energy is connected. Each of our bodies, too, is interconnected to all its parts. If one area of our body is out of balance, so is the rest of our body – whether we realize it or not. Think of stubbing your toe. We have all done that at one time or another. As a result of the pain, we walk with an abnormal gait, and probably with a limp. This puts strain on other parts of the body, which, in turn, affects even more parts. The cycle of such symptoms tells our body something is not right. It is our body announcing to us there is an energetic blockage someplace within.

* * * * *

Whether or not it has been processed, every emotion – along with its accompanying memories and beliefs and the experiences recorded by our senses, particularly smell – is stored in our subconscious mind. From conception to puberty, every sensory experience, whether positive or negative, is subconsciously absorbed and remembered and helps to create who we are as adults. Then, as adults, the process continues, yet now we have some life experiences to rationalize or understand some of those emotions; yet, they most likely will remain stuck.

It is important to note, then, that parents (particularly mothers), siblings, extended family members, teachers, religious leaders, societal leaders, and the media play a huge role in influencing the development of young minds.

To reiterate, every experience and emotion of the mother is absorbed into the subconscious mind of the developing fetus. The fetus takes in the energy of the environment, whether it is based on love or on fear. Again I bring up Baby Zoe. While still in the womb, she absorbed many negative emotions from her mother, particularly those about the unpleasant landlord. I also, as a seven-month fetus, picked up emotions from my mother when she found out she was having twins. How would I ever have known of these trapped emotions, which were affecting my very being, if I had not experienced an emotional release, by chance, at a metaphysical fair?

The subconscious does not know the difference between the present or past, whether you've seen something in a movie or experienced it in person, whether you've read it in a book and internalized it, or whether you've visualized something on your own. Yet, everything in the subconscious mind is real, and it is all in the here and now. In other words, it cannot distinguish between reality and imagination. In fact, your subconscious mind is so powerful you can manifest an image – if you hold it in your mind long enough – and if you feel it is real. This is what athletes, performers, and soldiers call visualization and what they do as part of their preparation and training. I used the same technique as a 12 year old in boarding school when I willed myself to feel well enough to attend a popular school play.

By the way, did you know the subconscious mind is approximately 90% of your mind, and it regulates every single cell in your body? It acts automatically to regulate the functioning of your organs and body systems. You cannot consciously control it.

The remaining 10% of your mind, with some believing the average person uses a maximum of between 1% and 5%, makes up your conscious mind.[5]

Imagine your mind as an iceberg...

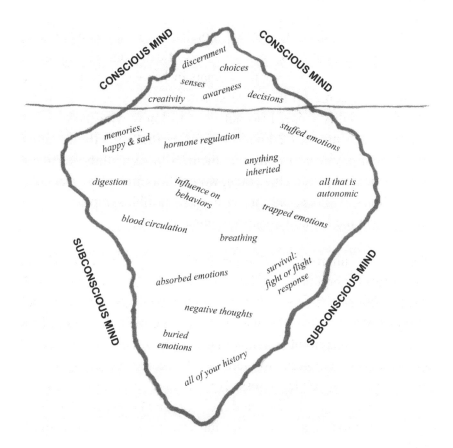

**The average human uses only 10% of their conscious mind....
That leaves roughly 90% of their subconscious mind operating
their bodies.**

*Note: This iceberg diagram is a simplified illustration of the
complexity of the mind. It is not intended to be scientifically accurate.*

How long does it take for these trapped emotions or energetic imbalances to manifest? Depending on the situation and the person, it can take only a few minutes for a symptom to manifest. Remember my experience with the gut punch feeling? I absorbed emotions from the man in the waiting room almost immediately.

However, it can take days, weeks, months, or years for imbalances to manifest as symptoms. In some cases, it can even take decades. I briefly worked with a young woman in her early twenties. The emotions that came up in the session told a story. Keep in mind, with any modality I use, I do not need to know why the client is coming to see me. All I know initially is that something, either emotional or physical, is bothering them. Although all the pertinent emotions occurred when the young woman was about two years old, it took almost two decades for her body to exhibit symptoms of the imbalance in the form of an autoimmune dis-ease.

Therefore, any unprocessed emotion, even if it may seem insignificant, can create an energetic imbalance – spiritual, emotional, or physical. When an imbalance occurs, it can manifest relatively soon as a cold, an ache, tight muscles, a headache, a dis-ease, irritability, or almost any physical, behavioral, or emotional symptom. There is no specific time frame for symptoms to manifest. To keep the energy flowing within the body, if you feel stressed out or out of sorts, a first step is to take a few slow, deep breaths and move around (walk, stretch). This may help you to refocus, thus allowing you to process your feelings, and avoid the creation of stuck or trapped emotions.

3. Conventional Healing

The doctor of the future will give no medication, but will interest his patients in the care of the human frame, in diet and in the cause and prevention of disease.

~ Thomas Edison

The world apparently has not yet reached Thomas Edison's future.

Conventional, Western, or allopathic doctors – those your health insurance will pay – still prescribe medication every single day. Let's look at a few definitions of conventional medicine.

Conventional medicine is, according to the *NCI Dictionary of Cancer Terms*, "...a system in which medical doctors and other healthcare professionals (such as nurses, pharmacists, and therapists) treat symptoms and diseases using drugs, radiation, or surgery. Also called allopathic medicine, bio-medicine, mainstream medicine, orthodox medicine, and Western medicine." [6]

The word allopathic comes from two Greek words: "állos," which means "other," and "pathos," which means "suffering." Samuel Hahnemann, the founder of homeopathy, coined the word "allopathic" in the early 19th Century for the practice of conventional medicine, and it is now commonly used.

A statement by Meredith Schweitzer, DO, adds to the definitions: "Conventional medicine is a medical model of evidence-based practice for diagnosing and treating disease." [7]

Given this statement alone, it is easy to see why the scientific world often claims that whatever cannot be seen by the naked eye or with a microscope does not exist. Because energy is not tangible it is often negated by conventional doctors.

* * * * *

In this book, I will use all three terms – conventional, Western, and allopathic – interchangeably.

A quick study of Western medicine and pharmaceutical companies over the last 100+ years shows that until the early 1900s, the practice of medicine was holistic. However, natural products from the earth cannot be patented; therefore, little money was, and is, to be made.

Enter John D. Rockefeller.

Rockefeller and his cohorts patented the chemical equivalent of Mother Nature's healing plants and began to make loads of money. Due to his influence in government and his control of the pharmaceutical companies [yes, he helped create the pharmaceutical companies], the practice of medicine began to change in dramatic ways. Eventually, the government, through the regulatory power of the United States Food and Drug Administration (USFDA or FDA), decreed that anything natural was to be banned and shunned. And so it all began: the infiltration of chemicals into our bodies to cure ailments. [8]

Around this time, the practice of chiropractic was also under attack. Many chiropractic schools were shut down by the government. Thankfully, some survived and the practice of chiropractic is making a solid comeback.

The disparity continues today, to the point the FDA all but frowns on successful healers and/or companies that offer natural or plant-based treatments. As a result, the modern version of Western medical education gives little to no time to alternative methods of healing. Instead, traditional medical students are trained at medical schools and universities with strong relationships with pharmaceutical companies.

Is it any wonder, then, that it is said "Western medicine is Rockefeller medicine"? [9]

Quite frankly, I find it scary to realize that our government will allow us to be and stay sick so that the powers that be can become wealthy from our purchases of their drugs. We are told to follow all our doctors' instructions, to do or to use what they tell us. If we think for ourselves, it becomes a problem – for them. According to F. Batmanghelidj, MD, "Patients continue to use [pharmaceuticals] because they are not cured. They are not *supposed* to be cured! They are only treated! This is the ideal way that commercialism in medicine can thrive." [10]

If open-minded patients, for example, inform their allopathic doctors they are doing something holistic or alternative for their care, the doctors, more often than not, will reprimand the patients. And it is not uncommon for a traditional doctor to rebuff or ridicule anything other than traditional medicine. Since the doctors are not trained in holistic medicine, the doctor will almost automatically counsel their patients against it. Having said this, I am personally beginning to notice that some doctors are becoming more accepting of holistic healing, even if they themselves do not practice it.

Please do not misunderstand me. I am for conventional medicine and doctors. There is a time and place for them. Some pharmaceuticals are lifesaving, and sometimes surgery is necessary. I utilize both types of doctors, traditional and alternative, for maintaining my health. If a bone is broken, I would go to the emergency room. However, if I have a basic sore throat, instead of first taking an over-the-counter medication, I would work on myself, doing emotional release healing, and utilize other holistic methods. Sometimes I may go to my primary care physician to clarify or identify what is ailing me. Then I would do what I can through energy healing before seeking further medical help.

Conventional, allopathic doctors can explain scientifically why a dis-ease has occurred and how cells have become maladaptive. Both usually happen as a result of long-term poor diet, lifestyle, or environment – but not always. Whenever diet, lifestyle or environment is not the cause, doctors tend to be at a loss for words, except to say the dis-ease is idiopathic, which means "unknown." Wikipedia adds "...with an apparently spontaneous origin..." [11]

With all due respect, I ask this question: Can these doctors tell you why those cells became maladaptive in the first place? Can they go beyond science to the initial root cause? Of course not. They cannot and/or will not admit the cause is an energetic imbalance in the body. Then, if a patient is cured for no "apparent" reason, heaven forbid the doctors say it is a miracle. They are dumbfounded and leave it at that, or they call it a "spontaneous remission."

There is a long-standing anecdote, the details of which change according to the teller, but the gist is the same. A patient goes to his doctor with a headache, and the doctor prescribes a drug to ease the patient's discomfort. The drug has side effects that cause the patient to feel tired. During his next visit, the patient complains about feeling tired. The doctor then prescribes yet another drug, one which ultimately gives the patient a headache. And so the cycle continues.

Years ago, when I worked in television, the only pharmaceuticals advertised were two different brands of aspirin and a stomach antacid. Now, the majority of commercials are promoting countless pharmaceuticals of one sort or another, even encouraging the viewer to ask their doctor if they ought to be taking the particular drug. However, all one needs to do is watch the pharmaceutical commercials on television to hear about the potential side effects. About 5 seconds of a 30-second commercial mentions the drug and its purpose. The remainder of the commercial warns the viewer of all the possible side effects, which may include death. The next time you watch such a commercial on television, time these two segments and see for yourself. It would be comical if it weren't so sad, and so true.

So, at one end of the spectrum, we have conventional medicine that primarily treats symptoms. At the other end is alternative, functional, holistic, or energy medicine that is centered on the origin of symptoms and treats the entire body, not just a part of it. Thus, although doctors on both sides want the same thing – to heal their patients – they come from differing perspectives, webs of belief. Herein lies the challenge: the two rarely meet in the middle. We, as a society can only wish and pray that the two approaches will someday work together.

4. Energy Healing

Energy healing has been around for thousands of years.
It comes in many forms.[12]

Energy healing, according to Francesca McCartney, PhD, in *A Brief History of Energy Medicine*, "....is bioelectric-based natural intelligence with a magnetic pull directing living organisms toward health. Any deviation from this innate attraction to grounded wellness creates disease." [13]

Ancient civilizations believed the body was a whole energy system that had an innate ability to heal itself. As time progressed, however, people came to believe that all the parts of the human body operated independently. Now modern scientists, as a result of many specialized studies, theorize that all matter is composed of energy and that the parts of the human body are indeed dependent on each other. Today, some in the healing profession say that our entire body is intelligent, not just our brain, and that our organs, including the heart, house individual intelligences that perform certain functions and produce specific emotions or feelings. It appears that healing theories and organ function theories have returned to the wisdom of ancient civilizations.

What I find intriguing is that, according to Chinese medicine, emotions happen in the body first. Then, the emotions occupy our minds. That is why ancient civilizations considered certain organs the seat of specific emotions. Dr. Bradley Nelson states in his book, *The Emotion Code,* that the ancient physicians were onto something when they observed that people who lived in anger tended to suffer from liver and gall bladder issues, those who lived in fear tended to suffer from bladder or kidney issues, and those who lived in grief tended to suffer from lung or colon issues.[14]

* * * * *

From my practice, research, and training, I've come to this realization: The client's religious faith is not a prerequisite for effective energy healing. What I find facilitates the healing is that one accepts we are spiritual beings having a human experience, believes there is a spiritual component to energy healing, or believes in a Higher Power or God. Having hope is imperative. Hope and faith are integral components of healing and expressions of your intention.

Energy healers tend to use the words "God," "Universe," "Source," "Spirit" or the "Divine" when they ask for assistance as they heal. I most often choose to use God or Universe and will do so in this book. No individual is a bona fide healer; each healer is but a conduit, or vessel, guided by God, to help a person heal. *This is what I believe.*

For years, and most typically in America, energy healing has been called quackery by non-believers. Also, until recently, there have been few successful scientific studies on energy or emotional healing because it is difficult to quantify and qualify all the variables involved, according to Gary Schwartz, PhD, in his book, *The Energy Healing Experiments.*[15]

Practitioners have adopted multiple terms to refer to energy healing. Energy medicine, spiritual healing, energy therapy, energy psychology, and emotional release healing are commonly used terms. Whatever one calls it, the healing takes place imperceptibly, and the results can be spontaneous or gradual. (One may not notice or feel a difference immediately, but may do so within hours or days.) Because energy is being moved around via the energy channels, such as the chakras and meridians, it appears to be invisible. However, the healing activates the body's subtle energy systems to remove energetic blockages. (Just as stuck energy creates imbalances in the body, so too is energy needed for healing.) Removing the blockages creates balance, and when the body is in balance, it has the innate ability to heal itself. Energy healing, in my humble opinion, goes beyond the physical aspect of the body, which is why it is so amazing.

> *In every culture and in every medical tradition before*
> *ours, healing was accomplished by moving energy.*
>
> ~ **Albert Szent-Gyorgyi** [16]

There are many different healing modalities, and they all work by moving energy in and around the body. Some are hands-on, some are hands-off, and some can even be done remotely. In other words, the practitioner and the client do not need to be in the same room, let alone the same country. While living in Florida, I have personally worked with clients who were in England, Australia, Canada, California, Illinois, Michigan, and Ohio, just to name a few places. The various healing modalities are just different ways of doing the same thing – moving energy around in order to release trapped negative energies within the body. One can choose any of the healing modalities, whichever resonates for that individual. Or, one can make use of more than one healing modality to assist the body in returning to balance. There is, after all, more than one route to a destination. *No judgment.*

Energy healing, no matter the modality used, enhances energy flow throughout a person's energetic field. Because every cell is designed for healing and regeneration, this movement of energy supports the self-healing ability of the body. When the body is put back into balance, it has the ability to heal itself. *A miracle.*

Following, in alphabetical order, are brief descriptions of some of the modalities that move energy in and around the body:

1. Access Consciousness® – Access Bars® is the very core of Access Consciousness®, developed and founded by Gary

Douglas in 1995, who was later joined by Dr. Dain Heer in 2000. According to Douglas, there are 32 points or bars of energy that run through and around the head, storing the electromagnetic component of all the thoughts, ideas, attitudes, decisions, and beliefs that you have ever had about anything. When the practitioner places their hands on specific points of your head, those points are activated and you are then able to release anything that does not allow you to receive your expanded consciousness. The "aim is to create a world of consciousness and oneness, where everything exists and nothing is judged." [17]

2. Acupuncture – Acupuncture works on balancing the body's energy fields. It involves inserting needles into the skin at specific points to alleviate discomfort and to treat various physical, mental, and emotional conditions. Originating in ancient China, acupuncture is now widely practiced in the West. Because needles are used, albeit extremely thin needles, one must be okay with being pricked multiple times and with having numerous needles simultaneously stuck in the skin for several minutes.

3. The Body Code – The Body Code is based on The Emotion Code yet is more comprehensive.[18] This advanced modality utilizes muscle testing to precisely locate the energetic imbalances within the body. The Body Code practitioner works with a specific computer program to pinpoint the indicated imbalances within the body, then passes a magnet either up or down the Governing Meridian a designated number of times to release the imbalance.

4. Chakra Healing – Also referred to as chakra balancing, chakra healing is based on the ancient Indian belief in a series of seven basic chakras, or energy centers, of the body. Chakra is Sanskrit for "wheel." The energy centers/wheels

are located at specific points between the base of the spine and the skull. Each energetic wheel has its own color and corresponds to specific areas of the body that regulate organ function, the immune system, and emotional aspects. When the chakras are balanced, energy and health is renewed.

5. The Emotion Code – Dr. Bradley Nelson, a holistic physician, devised this easy-to-use modality.[19] The practitioner references a chart of 60 emotions that are matched to the organs generally affected by, or storing, each emotion. By using muscle testing, the practitioner is able to connect to the client's subconscious mind to find and release the negative emotional energy that is manifesting as symptoms or imbalances. The practitioner passes a magnet either up or down the Governing Meridian a designated number of times to release the emotion.

6. Emotional Freedom Technique – "EFT" is also known as Tapping. Using the fingertips, a person taps a series of specific areas of the body's energy meridians, referred to as end points. While tapping, the person concentrates on the negative situation/emotion and then a positive affirmation.

7. The LifeLine Technique® – Dr. Darren R. Weissman, a holistic physician, developed this modality. "The cornerstone philosophy of The LifeLine Technique® is that symptoms, stress, and disease are the ways in which our bodies and lives speak to us to 'awaken' us to our authentic power to transform and create deep change."[20] The practitioner works with a detailed chart, one that serves as a blueprint of the subconscious mind and that pinpoints the location of the energetic imbalances within the mind and body. The practitioner uses muscle testing to communicate with the client's subconscious mind to find and release the source of imbalances and trapped emotions that manifest as symptoms and subconscious reactionary patterns.

8. Massage – Massage is the kneading and rubbing of the body's muscles, with the hands, to relieve tension or discomfort. Because massaging often releases trapped emotions, it is not uncommon for a client to weep as various muscles are massaged and relaxed.

9. Prayer – A prayer is a conversation with God (or one's personal definition of God) and serves as a means to ask for help, give thanks, or confess wrongdoing. A prayer can be said aloud or in your mind, formally, or free-flowing from your heart. [Prayer is a thought and a thought is energy, thus one is moving energy.]

10. The Reconnection – Dr. Eric Pearl, a chiropractor, is gifted with this modality of healing. He utilizes the universal intelligence accessible to all that brings our bodies into balance, without any "complex technique or elaborate ritual." [21]

11. Reflexology – By rubbing particular areas of the feet, hands, or ears – which correspond to various organs or systems in the body – reflexology stimulates those organs and systems, as well as the meridians. The meridians are like the superhighways of energy within the body.

12. Reiki – This spiritual healing art, of Japanese origin, was developed by Mikao Usui. The word Reiki means "universal life energy." The practitioner is connected to the Universe/Source and is aligned with their highest good, becoming a conduit for that energy to heal the client. The energy comes down through the head of the practitioner into their hands. Specific hand positions are placed either on or just above the client's body. The art of Reiki is passed down only through attunement. [22]

13. Toning/Sound Healing – Toning is a form of sound healing. It is an ancient modality in which the healer's voice is used,

sounding certain vowel sounds, notes, and tones. Each sound corresponds with, and is specific to, certain chakras, and is held for a certain number of minutes at the same pitch. Toning transforms the vibrational state of the body's cells, healing the negative stagnant energies.[23]

14. Yoga – Yoga is traditionally known as a Hindu spiritual, physical, and mental discipline. In contemporary Western society, it is used primarily as a form of exercise, meditation, and relaxation. There are multiple types of yoga practices, yet all incorporate and concentrate on awareness, breath control, specific body postures, and simple meditation. The root word for yoga is "yuj," which comes from Sanskrit and means "to join" or "to yoke." It can also mean "union."

15. The list goes on….

* * * * *

Energy healing with any modality may take only one session, or it may take multiple sessions. The number of sessions depends on the person and the situation. The bottom line is that the practitioner helps the client to release negative emotions, negative memories, life experiences, and feelings that are holding the client back or even creating physical or emotional pain or dis-ease. As the trapped energy is released, there is a possibility that the client may end up feeling more uncomfortable as the healing begins. This is called a healing crisis, and it is to be embraced and not feared. The crisis eventually subsides as the client's body processes the energy release.

At a weekend training for one of the modalities I practice, I was chosen from the audience of students to come on stage for a healing session by the doctor. Sometime in the wee hours of the morning, I felt myself scratching the palms of my hands. In my sleepy mind, I remembered how the class spent time outdoors and thought how odd for a mosquito to have bitten not one but both palms of my hands. However, when I awoke, there were no bug bites, but a rash covered both palms. The rash remained for almost two weeks. This was quite the healing crisis, with the emotional detox manifesting as the rash.

* * *

My work with Connor, who lives in England, is an example of a minor healing crisis. I worked with Connor remotely, removing a huge number of emotions, as much as his body allowed. A week later, when I asked him how he felt, he said he had been extremely tired the day after I worked with him. This example illustrates that, as energy moves, the client may sometimes feel "worse." In Connor's case, his healing crisis translated into sleeping more and only lasted 24 hours.

One thing is for sure. Releasing emotions is like tossing a pebble into a pond. You are the stone, and you create a ripple effect. Your newly acquired positive energy vibrations affect everyone with whom you come in contact.

Laurie had a roommate who was not a pleasant person. Laurie came to me to help her deal with her roommate. After we released a few of her emotions, our session was over. The next day, Laurie texted me to say her roommate was being exceptionally pleasant and had expressed a willingness to be a better roommate.

* * *

Another client, a middle-aged woman named Nadine, was experiencing challenges with every member of her family. She purchased a package of five sessions. At our second session, she commented that her husband was treating her better. At the third session, she said she had noticed a better relationship with her daughter. By the fourth session, we had released all the emotions that had initially been trapped. There was nothing left to release. I sent a few e-mail messages and made a few calls to remind Nadine she still had one more paid session, but Nadine never came back. She informed me she had nothing else to work on.

The following testimonial shows how powerful emotional release can be:

Many years ago, during an emotional release demonstration, I asked for a volunteer with a phobia or fear. I planned to show the power of emotional healing by finding and releasing only two emotions for that volunteer. Who knew that in a crowd of 40+ attendees, I would have trouble finding someone who would admit to having a fear or phobia. Eventually, one brave soul got up and came to the front of the room. Lucy had a fear of spiders. I inquired as to her level of fear, with zero meaning nothing and 10 being the worst. Her response was "Mine is a 20!" Using an Emotion Chart, I muscle tested Lucy to find the trapped emotions that were manifesting as her phobia. She was unable to relate to either of the two emotions. I then muscle tested for the age at which these emotions occurred. She could not relate to the age either. I then asked her how she would rate her fear of spiders. With great confidence, she held out her hand, pointed to her palm and declared, "You could place a spider right there, and I would be fine with it." Everyone in the room took that to mean the rating for her fear of spiders had gone down to zero. At the end of the presentation, she approached me and informed me that, at the age I had found, she had been driving her car when a spider had come down from the roof, right in front of her face, and had almost caused her to lose control of her car. She was so appreciative to be rid of her fear.

* * * * *

I have practiced or experienced all of the aforementioned modalities, with excellent results. I became aware of Reiki and was intrigued by it for many years before I "awakened" to other energy work. Reiki was the first healing modality I studied, other than yoga and prayer. Becoming attuned in Reiki, for me, was the most significant aspect of the modality. When I got attuned, I immediately felt the energy running through my body, especially through my hands. I practiced Reiki briefly, but quite honestly - and I hesitate to admit this for there are some Reiki practitioners who live and breathe Reiki - once I learned it, it did not hold my interest. I did not care for standing up with my arms outstretched for the entire session, which can last for at least 30 minutes.[24] Therefore, Reiki took its place as one of the first stepping stones in my quest for healing modalities and knowledge.

Although I gained valuable and useful skills with both Reiki and Access Consciousness, the modalities that appealed to me most are The Emotion Code and The LifeLine Technique®. They both find and release specific emotions. (Plus, I find I can utilize either one even while I'm out walking or otherwise out of my office – very user friendly.) I have yet to find any other healing modality that works with emotions in the way these two modalities do. Since emotions are vibrations, and vibrations are energy, they are also referred to as emotional release healing modalities, not just energy healing modalities.

Because I practice these two similar modalities, occasionally I am asked about the differences between them. They are both powerful healing modalities. I like them equally. They both find and locate the trapped subconscious emotions, reactionary patterns, and the imbalances within the body that manifest as physical or emotional symptoms, and I find that they can complement each other. Both modalities are referred to as "content free," which means the client need not share personal information. Holistic practitioners of these two modalities are not shrinks (psychiatrists) and do not engage in rehashing the traumas or issues of the client because, in this work, rehashing the past only serves to reinforce what the client is attempting to release. Having said this, it is still helpful for the client to share a small amount of personal information with the practitioner so that the practitioner can effectively guide the session. That issue would then be "revisited" only to compare the client's feelings at the end of the session to those the client had at the beginning.

With The Emotion Code, the client shares what they wish to address, either physically or emotionally. If they do not wish to share, they can just say "mystery symptom." The practitioner, using muscle testing, and asking specific questions requiring only a "yes" or "no" response, finds the trapped emotions and releases them. Because The Emotion Code chart has 60 emotions listed, the practitioner can easily locate the emotion ready to be released by following the technique. The client tells the practitioner whether or not any of the released emotions, and occasionally accompanying ages, resonate with them. Whatever the answer, it is okay, because the client's subconscious mind will let the practitioner and client both know if that bit of information is necessary to know.

With The Body Code, an advanced version of the Emotion Code, the practitioner, using a special computer program, asks if there are any energetic imbalances. Through muscle testing, if the response is "yes," the practitioner then continues through the program following prompts to get to the source of the imbalances, then releases it/them. [It reminds me of a treasure hunt.]

With The LifeLine Technique®, clients sit in what I compassionately and understandably refer to as the "hot seat" as they are actively involved in their healing. The practitioner uses a detailed chart considered a blueprint of the subconscious mind, to find and release trapped emotions and subconscious reactionary patterns. In addition, with the guidance of the practitioner, the client creates a positive intention of how they would rather feel, as if they are already there. Because the intention is harmonized with the client's subconscious mind, I believe that creating an intention with this modality is different than merely reading one from a book. With The LifeLine Technique®, your intention becomes personalized and internalized.

Another distinction to the LifeLine Technique® is the repeated use of the words "infinite love and gratitude" throughout a session, as well as signing "I love you" using the American Sign Language (ASL) symbol. That symbol is, unto itself, a healing modality.

What is so kool about releasing trapped emotions is that once one finds and releases an emotion, particularly one that is inherited, it is released not only from you, but from all your ancestors of the affected lineage and your current and future children. As the saying goes, "The buck stops here." Those negative emotions and memories have been cellularly released (released negative memories from your cells), raising your vibration, clearing the way for a better you.

I also work with Young Living essential oils. Essential oils are aromatic, volatile (evaporate easily) oils extracted from flowers, seeds, shrubs, roots, trees, or bushes.[25] In centuries past, essential oils were used to heal practically every ailment, as well as to embalm bodies. Modern research has proven the powerful healing capacity of high quality essential oils. The oils help one return to the fundamentals of healing, the way Mother Nature intended healing to be – natural. What I like about high quality essential oils is that, because they are natural, the plants creating the oils grow according to their environment. The combination of factors such as soil, growing conditions, geographic region, and climate differ slightly with every growing season, thus preventing bad microorganisms from adapting.[26] In addition, most viruses, bacteria, and fungi cannot live in the presence of most essential oils.[27] Pharmaceuticals, on the other hand, require precise standardization and are thus produced under the same conditions year after year. This gives bad germs time to genetically modify and become immune to many synthetic, pharmaceutical drugs. I also like these oils because I believe the founder of Young Living Essential Oils, Dr. D. Gary Young, has set the highest standards for essential oil purity and authenticity. The oils are carefully monitored throughout the production process – from seed to seal.

I like, and use, (especially the water system) Nikken's wellness products. These wellness products help the body get into balance, and thus on the road to health. Just writing this reminds me of two stories about how using these products convinced Tony, my husband, of their value, quality, and effectiveness.

First Tony Story: When we lived in Italy, years before my "awakening" to emotional release healing, Tony partook in a group skiing trip to the Abruzzo Mountains while I was in Poland shopping for Polish pottery. After the group left the slopes, Tony somehow wrenched his knee. The next day he miraculously managed to get himself to the military base hospital where the doctor gave him unwelcome news. The doctor informed Tony there was no way he would be able to participate in the Rome marathon he had planned to run in a few weeks. That was the wrong thing to tell my husband. Bound and determined to run in that race, Tony became the embodiment of *intention.* When Tony returned to our villa, he asked himself, "What would Susan do to take care of me?" He then used every

Nikken magnet and bio ceramic wrap we had. A few weeks later, my husband ran, and completed, the Rome marathon, the *Maratona di Roma*. Although he ended up with a popped blister that bloodied his sock, Tony had no issues with his knee during the race! After the race, I helped him hobble over to the first aid tent. There, oh my gosh, the medical personnel poured – yes, poured – alcohol on the open blister. My husband, the stoic military guy, just grimaced a little and chuckled. Later, as Tony hobbled, and I walked back to the hotel, he said, "If our roles were reversed, they would have heard you cussing across the ocean." *True.*

Second Tony Story: A couple of years later, back in America on a Holy Thursday, Tony was driving to work in the white BMW he loved, a car he had bought before we left Italy. A speeding pickup truck plowed into the rear of Tony's car and pushed it into the car in front of Tony. That car then hit the car in front of it, and the result was a four-vehicle pileup. After I picked him up from the hospital, I "Nikkened" Tony up by wrapping him in every Nikken magnet and bio ceramic wrap we had. I made sure to cover all his bruises, welts, and aching muscles. All I could see was his head, mostly covered in magnets, and the black stretchy material of the bio ceramic wraps. He looked so funny I have regretted many times not taking a photo of him. Anyway, by Easter Monday, he was back at work with no visible signs of having been in an accident. No bruises. No welts. No limping. We were full of *gratitude* that Tony had not been seriously injured – and that these wellness products had helped his body return to balance and heal more quickly than it would have had by conventional methods.

5. Why Some May Say Energy Healing Does Not Work

It is the fear of change that keeps people stuck in a cycle of pain and suffering.[28]

~ **Neal Burgis, PhD**

The question is not whether or not energy healing works. It does. The question is whether or not a person really wants, consciously or subconsciously, to get better.

Some shun energy healing because their allopathic doctors do not recommend it (as a result of their doctors not being aware of it or not being taught about it in medical school).

There is a parable, urban legend, tall tale, analogy – call it what you will – that I refer to as the froggy-in-the-water phenomenon. If a froggy is placed directly in hot water, the froggy will jump out. If, however, the froggy is placed in a container of cold water, and the water temperature is gradually increased, the froggy will most likely remain in the container. This happens because the froggy's internal thermostat adjusts to the warming temperature, reducing its sensitivity to discomfort or pain. In time, the froggy dies as it boils to death.

Alan Cohen uses the concept of "drift" to explain how this could happen.[29] Drift is a slow and gradual movement from one place or condition to another. Using this definition, the froggy analogy can be applied to human behavior. If we become adjusted to a harmful situation – e.g., one lacking in love or one full of conflict – we have reduced our sensitivity, just like the froggy, to the effects of our environment. In time, we are no longer able to hear our inner self speak to us, to recognize that our body, our mind, our spirit, is telling us we are out of balance.

Often, then, we may feel more comfortable dealing with our current discomfort than we are learning to experience something never felt – even if that something is a feeling of peace, love, or belonging. And the longer we continue in discomfort, the harder it may be to feel comfortable enough to release the trapped emotions. Entering any "strange" realm of feeling – even if the feeling is positive – can be scary.

Prior to a young child's healing session, she drew and colored at a small table. Her shoulders were hunched and her hands quivered. After her session, she resumed drawing and coloring. Her hands did not quiver, and I could sense her body was more at peace. But soon she remarked aloud, in a concerned tone, "Whoa! Something is different!" Within hours, her shoulders were again hunched and her hands quivered. The positive feelings she had felt were too foreign for her to maintain because she lived in an environment where love and affection were not readily available.

* * *

As I worked through the process of certification for one of the modalities I work with, I asked practically everyone I knew if I could practice with them. One lady agreed but with hesitation. Trish was a middle-aged woman, and her declared issue was feeling stuck in life. We scheduled a session, and at the end, we revisited how she felt. I was expecting a huge improvement because of the emotions released. To my utter amazement, and this was a first for me, she responded that she felt the same. She stated she would rather remain in the emotional quagmire she was in than make a conscious choice to change. Trish admitted she had told her weight-loss mentor the same thing. So, I was not alone in making a heartfelt choice to help Trish feel better, an effort to no avail. She did, however, ask me to work with her dog, which I did with success. Years later, I ran into Trish. She was still stuck – and still not willing to make changes.

Among those unwilling to change are people who subconsciously like the attention they receive as a result of their physical or emotional situation.

When I visited an elderly man, almost immediately he eagerly showed me all his medicines and medical equipment and informed me of all the doctors who were treating him. Why should he get better? He was getting a lot of attention because of his ill health. If he got healthy, he'd be just one of the crowd.

* * *

When I initially got involved with Nikken products, I met a lady in the waiting room at a military base clinic. She appeared to be in immense discomfort, so I offered to introduce her to the magnetic and bio ceramic wrap products of Nikken. She was open. I contacted a mentor, Naomi, who lived close by and who is trained in psychology and the medical field. As a neophyte, I wanted Naomi to go with me to this lady's house to assist me in engaging her in experiencing specific products for her needs. In the middle of the experiential demonstration, Naomi mouthed to me that we would be leaving soon, and she shortened the presentation. As we returned to our car, Naomi explained to me that the lady did not want to get better. Astonished and flabbergasted, I asked Naomi how she could possibly know that. Naomi informed me that, as we worked with her, the lady's muscles were relaxed, and she mentioned how relaxed she felt. However, whenever one or more of her family members entered the room, the lady's muscles would tense up, as if on cue, and she would begin to comment on how much discomfort she was in. Then, after the family members left the room, her muscles again relaxed. Naomi commented that, although we were there to share the wellness products, which could assist her body to take care of itself, the lady was so in need of her family's sympathy and attention, she would probably never benefit from the products. I learned a lot from that event.

Some people may not want to upset the family dynamics.

I received a call from a middle-aged man who hesitantly stated he needed help. He did not specify why. [The beauty of the modalities I practice is that clients do not need to give me specifics. In fact, they may refer to their issues as "mystery issues."] During his session, we released many emotions. The age at which these emotions first got stuck told the story that something significant had occurred at that time. I do my best to refrain from telling clients they "should" do something, so I suggested, if possible, it would be in his best interest to speak with his mother. He replied that he could, but he did not want to disturb her. He then clammed up. Before he left, he shared that he had worked with someone in the city nearby, and her energy work had failed him. As he described her, I realized she was a colleague, so I later contacted her about him. Without skipping a beat, she stated we ought not to work with this man because he wanted others to fix his life for him. She believed there was very little that any emotional or energy healer could do to help him. Despite making a follow-up appointment with me, he canceled it the day before we were to meet – which led me to concur with my colleague's conclusions.

For whatever reason, some folks may not want to come to grips with their past. I have multiple stories about such clients; however, I will share just one.

My husband and I were working at a metaphysical fair. Betsy waited over 30 minutes for me while I worked with another client. Betsy was pleasant enough, yet when she sat down, I instinctively knew this was going to be an interesting session, in that Betsy was going to be challenging, but not intentionally. Even though I followed all the protocols of the two modalities with which I work, including prayer, she was unable to identify with any of the emotions I found – even when I also "found" the ages in which they were stuck. Her facial expression was blank, despite her insistence she wanted to feel better. Finally, I thought that, perhaps, my husband could better connect with her. He worked with her for a long time, too, and eventually informed her that neither one of us could help her. After she left, we were exhausted and agreed our results with her were negligible. Later, her daughter came by and informed us that Betsy was on antidepressants and multiple pharmaceuticals, which when combined, blunted her ability to feel emotions. Apparently, she was unable, consciously or subconsciously, to release anything from her past, with or without her medications.

Some people, as sad as it may be, may simply prefer to live with their issues. Their issues somehow spur them on or give them a reason to live.

Maggie came to me because her mother hoped I'd be able to help her. No one, no matter what their training, had been able to help Maggie thus far. Now a young adult, Maggie revealed she had been attacked, raped, and beaten by several guys when she was preadolescent. She told no one about the experience for years, not even her parents. The story was heartbreaking and horrifying. After two extremely difficult sessions (for me), all we had been able to release were a couple of emotions. I dreaded having to inform her mother I could not help Maggie. All Maggie wanted to do was find the mystery men and torture them. She harbored such anger and hate that anything to do with healing was pointless. Her deep desire to inflict pain on the mystery men overshadowed any positive efforts others made to help her deal with the trauma.

Some individuals are raised in, or live in, such a negative environment that all they know is to feel poorly about themselves and their lives. They are taught, or conditioned, not only to feel few emotions but also to feel unworthy. In order not to be disappointed by anyone or anything, they do not aim high. What a foreign, fearful life they live, but they cannot imagine it any other way. In fact, to be happy or to feel worthy is meant for someone else, not them, so they do not even venture into the possibilities of a different life.

I attempted to work with an older female acquaintance. She was married to, by all accounts, a horrible man. From what I heard, his adult children were also nasty and never respected her or accepted her as their dad's second wife. She had been miserable for decades yet refused to leave him due to her religious beliefs. I asked her to create an intention of how she would rather feel, as if she were already feeling it. All she would say, over and over, was, "This won't work." She could not fathom feeling any other way than rejected, disrespected, and unloved. And, yes, she had health challenges. To preserve my professional dignity and integrity, I had to step aside and cease working with her.

Many people wish to clearly identify with their social circle, and because of that, some refuse to make any changes that would make them "different." They want so badly to participate in the common drama they would rather remain with their issues than change. And, for some, it is very much "in" to complain about everything in life. If they do not complain, they fear they will become an outsider to their group of friends.

Sadly, this is a common occurrence. I've had people tell me it is okay with them to have a particular phobia (for example) because without it they would have nothing to be concerned about, nothing to talk about. This is an important point. What if a person's symptom or phobia is released? Who would the person be? What would their "story" be? What would their identity be?

Some individuals express concern that energy healing may interfere with or go against their faith. Despite the explanation that we are energy and everything around us is energy, these folks still refuse this type of healing.

In one case, a mother was concerned about giving her baby drugs for an allergy. Although she was a pharmacist who knew well the negative side effects of the drugs, she still preferred pharmaceuticals to the perfectly safe energy healing – because she believed energy healing conflicted with the Bible.

One woman who suspected she was unable to metabolize certain foods was eager for me to muscle test her for those foods. The more we spoke, the more it became apparent she was actually afraid that energy work would go against her faith. She fervently believed if something was not written specifically in the Bible, she should not participate.

> *If you really want something, you'll find a way. If you don't, you'll find an excuse.*
>
> ~ **Emanuel James "Jim" Rohn**

What I, as well as other healers, have noticed is that many people do not want to do the work of energy healing (where "work" means such things as acknowledging their emotions, taking responsibility for their lives, or even uncovering deeply buried hurtful memories). They would rather have a psychic or intuitive tell them nice things about their lives than to get to the origin of their personal issues. (I am not disparaging psychics or intuitives in any way.)

Some folks need the ego, the conscious mind, to be in charge. Because they cannot imagine anything being "wrong" with them, their ego says they are fine. They either "know it all," or they do not wish to hear of another way to do anything. However, their attempt to retain control through their ego may eventually be upended. As they get out of balance, reality takes over and their bodies begin to manifest symptoms. This may, or may not, convince them to relinquish the power of their ego. Due to the Law of Free Will, no one can *make* them get healthier; they must *want* and *choose* to become healthier.

Occasionally, at the beginning of a first healing session, clients (or shall I say, their egos) say they know what emotions will come up. They think they have it all figured out, but the subconscious mind has other plans. When their "chosen" emotions do not come up during the first session, a few conclude emotional healing is quackery and may not wish to return for another session. If they do continue, however, they discover, much to their surprise, other emotions needed to be released first. In time, they realize their conscious self, their ego, is not in control; their subconscious is in control.

They also learn it is not in their best interest to overanalyze. At the very beginning of my learning curve, as I partook in my first class ever on emotional release, I was told over and over by both the doctor and the facilitators not to overanalyze. I was offended and shocked. I wanted to figure it all out. I wanted to understand it, every last detail of it. Even if I did not comprehend the scientific aspects, I needed to find a connection of some sort. But I learned, as everyone does, there is no need to analyze, let alone doubt, whatever comes up. *Anything can cause anything. It is what it is.*

A final point: It's in the best interest of healer and client alike to just go with the flow.

6. Barriers to Emotional Healing

Everyone is about as happy as they make up their mind to be.

~ **Abraham Lincoln**

The only thing we are ever dealing with is a thought, and a thought can be changed.[30]

~ **Louise Hay**

What are your priorities when it comes to getting healthier? Choose carefully because modern-day priorities are skewed.

When I worked at a network television station in New York City, my job was to place commercials, billboards, public service announcements, and the correct episodes for programs. The products in the commercials consisted primarily of cereals, baby food, toys, American-made cars and trucks, foreign-made cars and trucks, and two brands of aspirin. In contrast, a major portion of today's commercials advertise pharmaceuticals that seem to have more damaging side effects than benefits.

Many of today's television programs are reality shows that pit one person against another, inane comedies, or programs with seriously negative or violent undertones. The result is a steady stream of negative, derogatory, or snide comments emanating from our viewing devices. The few programs that are educational often have narrators who speak in such an urgent, dramatic fashion, I feel they detract from the value of the program.

An antidote is to watch old movies, even if their lack of computer-generated action and sound effects make them seem boring. Observe the politeness used by the characters and the respect they showed to others. Even the bad guys were decent. Observe the style of clothing and how the everyday person dressed up for everyday situations.

A couple of years after working in network TV, I worked in the newsroom of an affiliate TV station. I learned so much from the news director. *Gratitude.* Jim was a no-nonsense news director. When he first arrived at the station, he held a mandatory meeting for the newsroom staff. He pointed out the ways television news was currently being delivered, locally and nationally. He instructed the reporters to correct their terminology and delivery so that everything was factual and not redundant, not assumptive, and not editorialized. *Bravo.* I also learned that society, for centuries (yes, centuries), has gravitated first to dramatic, even violent, news stories rather than to feel-good stories. *Sad.*

The American media have us programmed into wanting more and more stuff. Just stuff. We, as a society are bombarded with the need for bigger, wider TV screens; fancier cars; and a particular coffee drink, not just once in the morning but throughout the day. The list goes on. America has evolved into one of the most wasteful countries in the world. I promote the idea that all high school or college students take the opportunity to do a semester abroad in a third-world country or in an impoverished area of America. When people see only their immediate world, they tend not to appreciate what they have or to comprehend how others, less fortunate, live. *Very myopic.*

Modern society has also created an environment where we are all not only dependent on electronic technology, but many of us are also hooked on it. In addition, too many people are getting their facts from sound bites, blogs, or short videos, and not doing their own research. I believe the result is a lack of critical thinking and a self-absorbed society. Manners, morals, ethics, respect, kindness, and plain decency seem to be lacking, creating many of the social ills we have today. Generally speaking, people seem to know more about their rights than they do about their responsibilities to society, with apathy becoming the norm. Please understand, although I am referring to the apparently new norm in this day and age, I acknowledge and am grateful for all the goodness that does exist in society.

Once, while traveling in Eastern Europe, I noticed a train with several hands and arms hanging out the windows. Referring to this sight, I asked my European companion what would happen if someone was seriously injured? The response? "Oh, well. They know better than to do that, but they're taking the chance. This is not sue-happy America." This European attitude about Americans illustrates how we have developed into a society that commonly blames others for our errors, as well as a me-first culture, often concerned more about our cell phones and texting than we are about actually speaking with one another. *What? You didn't get my text? I'll just message you.*

The media inundate us with messages to seek external fulfillment from someone or something outside our personal lives. Why? Appealing to our wants and "needs" is good marketing and sells products and services. As a result, too many folks believe they truly do need all kinds of stuff to be happy. [For example, I once overheard a teenager exclaim to his parents, whether or not in jest, that he could not live without the shiny electronic device in the store window.] So, folks buy and buy, and, before they realize it, they are deeply in debt. They then take on another job to pay the bills, spending less time at home with friends and family. The result is a feeling of emptiness, despite their cell phones, nice wardrobes, cars, and other stuff. To fill the void, they buy more stuff and go into more debt. The cycle becomes never ending. What a breeding ground for trapped emotions.

If people are constantly distracting themselves (with television, headphones, video games, cell phones, and so forth) – without taking time out to relax and replenish the body and the mind – they will end up reacting to life rather than living life consciously. And, when they are in a state of reaction all the time, chances are they are not happy, whether or not they are aware of their unhappiness. So, if any one person is reacting as a way of living, that person may be unable to feel an emotion. If they feel an emotion, it may be expressed as anger or frustration. And, if one cannot feel an emotion, how can one heal? Occasionally, I have clients who, when asked how they would rather feel, as in being in a happier state of mind, they just offer a blank expression. They are unable to feel anything.

What one must acknowledge, first and foremost, is the difference between two types of happiness: emotional-peace-of-mind happiness versus how-much-stuff-I-have happiness. Which is really better? Which truly brings lasting happiness? The media, unfortunately, seldom offer the message that happiness, true happiness, comes from within. We do need all the basics – shelter, food, and clothing. And, yes, we all want certain things for a more comfortable life. But when our wants get out of control, the problems begin. We must look within for happiness – and for healing. Self-fulfillment comes from within. Ask anyone who volunteers who benefits most from their work. Is it the volunteer or those who are served? [If you, the reader, do not volunteer, or have never volunteered, give it a try.]

Again, the bottom-line question is this: What are your priorities for living a happier life? For becoming healthier? Is it more important to keep up with your "neighbors", to buy what the media tell you to buy to feel special? This will provide some short-term happiness. Or are you willing to forgo the excess stuff and make the commitment to heal yourself, either physically or emotionally, or both, which ultimately provides long-term happiness?

Take care of you the way you take care of your favorite possession. There is only one you.

> *Happiness is the meaning and the purpose of life,*
> *the whole aim and end of human existence (...)*
> *Happiness depends upon ourselves.*

> ~**Aristotle**

7. How My Life Has Shifted

You can never cross the ocean unless you have the courage to lose sight of the shore.

~ Christopher Columbus

The shift certainly did not occur overnight. It has taken years of learning and experience, gained through education and through trial and error, to get to where I am now. Yet, I know I have a ways to go, as I am always evolving...because change is the essence of life.

I now understand that we come into this world with lessons to learn as well as lessons to teach.

I am more at ease. I am more open to ideas. I own up to failures more quickly because, if not, ego gets in the way of enjoying life fully. Just because I may fail at a task doesn't mean I am a failure. Most successful people have failed at one time or another. In fact, they probably failed more than one time. Failing is a learning step. Live and let learn.

I am more discerning about what I watch on TV. I have come to believe that much of what is important to the mainstream media is ridiculous or unimportant in the larger picture of life. Advertisers, news announcers, program hosts, just about all the voices in media these days, speak with a definitive urgency to attract listeners. Because hype goes a long way, the loudest, chattiest person seems to get the most attention. However, does that make what they have to say more worthwhile? Not always. When I grew up, and I'm dating myself here, we had only three national networks. Programming was in black and white for years before color became the norm. If we wished to change the TV channel, we had to get off the chair, walk to the TV, and turn the knob by hand. News reports were delivered in a professional and matter-of-fact manner, and – I'm assuming – a more unbiased viewpoint. Now, there are hundreds, if not thousands of programs and channels that offer entertainment and escapism. Some, I feel, even come close to demeaning one's intelligence.

When I'm on the road, if there is some jerk driving like a maniac, I let them be. I no longer feel the need to stand my ground. I allow them to get ahead. Better ahead of me than behind me, that is for sure. I think of the Socrates quote, "Be kind, for everyone you meet is fighting a hard battle." *One never knows....*

I am more empathic, and as I continue on my life path, I find myself becoming more intuitive.

I can no longer spend any length of time with folks who see only negativity.

Although I am still hard on myself (aiming to be the very best I can be), I am not as hard on myself as I used to be, thank goodness. I do not doubt *every* move I make, every decision I make. For years, and I mean years, as in most of my younger life, I always doubted my choices. One day, while living in Sacramento, I went to see a psychic/intuitive woman. It was a weird experience. I drove one hour out into the country to meet with her in an RV parked outside her house, a setting that made me feel like I was in a cult movie. The RV had not been used in a while, and there were more than a few cobwebs in the corners. I entered, and before I could even wipe the dust off the bench, the woman started talking, as if she had just returned from taking a break. She talked without preamble, leaving out the typical fanfare of an initial intuitive reading – a small prayer, a moment of silence, a holding of hands. It was a minute or so before I comprehended she was speaking about a recent past life, apparently, my most recent past life. Until that moment, I had never given past lives much thought as the concept was neither a part of my upbringing nor of my religious education. But what she was saying made sense to me because it explained why I had always doubted myself. In the other life she spoke of, I had been in charge of a military covert rescue team. Just as we were about to rescue our subject, one of my hand-picked men murdered me. How could I have missed the fact he was a traitor? How could I have made such a mistake? Wow. Those dramatic and traumatic last-second emotions became trapped prior to my death, and that past life was still manifesting in my current life as self-doubt. Having this particular past life, I suspect, also explained why I was drawn to Fort Ord, the Army base in Monterey, California, the first time I drove past it. [Fort Ord has since closed down as a base.]

I trust that we are all on our own path, a path that we agreed to in the Akashic Records (also known as the Book of Life). If someone cannot be healed by any method known to healers or allopathic doctors, then I believe it is their path in this life not to be healed. It may sound callous, yet this way of thinking helps me make sense of someone's illness or death if I cannot comprehend it. It also helps me in my grieving process.

For a few years, I was chairman of a committee and had a lot of responsibilities. Along with the responsibilities came a lot of stressors. Occasionally I was hard on myself, doubting myself, and rehashing my words and decisions. Thankfully I had the tools to recognize what was occurring within, and work on myself energetically. *Immense gratitude.*

Two points concerning this experience stand out. One day, while doing work for the committee, I made a computer error with the slip of the hand and was more than upset with myself. In my mind, it was an intense "oops". I was unable to gather my composure to work energetically on myself so I called a fellow committee member. Wise woman she was. She calmly said, "What is done is done." She then added, "Maybe it was meant to be." I felt like an angel had come down and spoken the exact words I needed to hear. I call it "a God thing." Bells went off in my head. Oh, my, gosh. Talk about an immediate shift. Wow. I became calmer at once and felt the angst literally leave my body. *What happens is meant to be.* I realized I already knew this. Even so, it was reaffirming to have her remind me of this Universal truth.

The other point I want to share is that once I asked for guidance from Above, from God, about the chairmanship position, I was able to see more clearly. I was at peace. I was also able to realize that this position was a learning experience for me – almost a test to see how I have actually grown in living my talk. *Gratitude on many counts.*

I often take a step back in my mind, now that I'm no longer on the committee, and realize how valuable my emotional release training has been. What if I had not chosen to live in gratitude? How differently would I have responded to the many challenges? What if I had not "awakened" to realizing that I am a spiritual being having a human experience? What if I did not know we are on this earth to learn lessons – as well as to help others with their lessons? Wow. *Gratitude for my life's path.*

This brings me to yet another point about how I have shifted my way of thinking and thus changed my life. I do not believe things happen by coincidence, even though I occasionally use that word. The concept of coincidence has become a common notion in our society. As odd or as harsh as it may sound, though, I really do believe there are no random events, no coincidences. I believe, instead, there is a larger plan for life than any of us can imagine. As humans, we tend to believe that we are in control of our lives. In actuality, it is God who is in control. His control is called Divine Providence, and He operates in *kairos* time (His appointed time), not *chronos* time (our human chronological time).

Following is a lovely example of Divine Providence:

Right after my siblings and I buried our mother's ashes in Chicago, we decided to visit our only remaining relative from her generation, her cousin Felicia. Barbara and I liked Felicia and had our minds set on visiting her. The challenge was that she was in the hospital recuperating from surgery. One of Felicia's daughters was a nurse, and she had suggested to Kathy, her sister, that it might be too much for their mom to receive so many visitors (6, to be precise) at this time. Nonetheless, Kathy, Barbara, and I decided we would all go to the hospital. Our plan was that Kathy would go upstairs first to see her mom and inquire if we could actually visit. Meanwhile, the rest of us would remain in the lobby. With this plan in mind, we walked across the parking lot toward the hospital entrance. Right before we reached the door, we spotted a car with a personalized license plate that read "Irene." Irene was my mother's name! With huge grins, Kathy, Barbara, and I all high-fived each other, realizing this was a sign from Above that we were to visit Felicia in the hospital. And our visit made everyone's day. Although we had never done it before, since that time, Felicia and I have made regular telephone calls to each other. I cherish those phone conversations immensely. Gratitude.

Here is an example of being connected, and, of listening to one's inner voice. This is actually my sister's story:

When our Mom was in rehab following her major stroke, Barbara was in the condo one night putting away Christmas decorations. She heard an inner voice softly say, "Go." Silently, to herself, she replied, "I will once I get these decorations put away." A minute or so later, the inner voice was stronger. "Go!"

Her inner response was the same. Another minute or so later, the inner voice was heard again, this time definitely firm. "GO!!!!" Barbara's response, in her head, was "All right already. Let me put my outdoor shoes on first." Then off she went to the rehab facility. By this time it was late in the evening, long after the rehab facility had locked its front doors for the night. Using the special nighttime code to enter, Barbara dashed to Mom's room. She found Mom half off the bed, with a frightened and pained look on her face, unable to communicate due to the effects of the stroke. No telling how long Mom had been that way. She was fine when Barbara was with her at dinner time. And no telling what would have happened to her if Barbara had not heard that inner voice and listened to it. There was no aide in sight.

The more one understands, even in a basic way, that everyone and everything is energy – and thus connected – the easier life becomes. However, if one believes we live in a physical universe – not an energy-based universe – the more difficult life may appear to be. Have you ever attempted to go after a goal and never succeeded? The effort can be as futile as mankind attempting to control the weather. Chances are the lack of success is a message from God/Universe directing us elsewhere so we can return to our life's path. On the other hand, what does it mean if we go after some goal and life just flows? It means we are congruent with our life's path. *Gratitude.*

Here is a personal experience that serves as a good example of God/Universe having a plan for us that we may have never considered:

When I was living in Sacramento, I desired a different, more exciting job than the one I had. I was working in the business office of a TV station but wanted to work in one of the other departments. I applied for several, but it was not to be. I then applied outside the station for jobs, some of which felt like they were custom made for me. Still, I did not even get interviewed. Needless to say, I was depressed and frustrated, and developed a deep lack of self-worth. Then, I received a phone call. I was being recruited to work at a TV station in Monterey. I accepted the job, and, one year later, I met Tony, the man who was to become my husband. Years later, when I looked back on my life, I had such an "ah-ha" moment. All the struggles made sense. I had not gotten any of those "perfect" jobs because God's plan for me was to meet Tony in Monterey! If I had gotten any one of them, as I had hoped, I never would have met Tony. In my eyes, God's plan for me was as plain as day.

Yes, we do have free will to make conscious choices, to direct our lives. We can make all kinds of detailed plans, but if that is not what God/Universe has planned for us, our plans will go amok. One person's *choice* to do something horrific, let's say, can ultimately have a snowball effect on strangers. I have no solid answer for *why* horrible things happen. I wish I did. Why did my cousin have to be killed by a drunk driver (who, due to political connections only spent a token amount of time in jail) just as my cousin was getting his life in order? Why did I have to have three surgeries on one hip only to still struggle to do ordinary things? (By the way, being stuck in this type of "why" mindset is a negative/low vibration.) Many who have witnessed my long recovery process tell me I am an inspiration for perseverance after adversity. So, you see, observing my struggles may benefit others who also struggle and help them to carry on. That may just be part of the larger plan of life, and of my life. *The Celestine Prophecy*, a book by James Redfield, is a great introduction to the there-is-no-coincidence philosophy. Knowing all this, it is easier to go with the flow of life and to enjoy the ride. I take comfort in believing that the medical personnel who were responsible for the hip situation will have *a lot* of explaining to do when they reach "the pearly gates." *It is what it is. Carry on.*

I can't help but think of the Shakespearian quote from "As You Like It," Act II, Scene VII: "All the world's a stage, And all the men and women merely players. They have their exits and their entrances, And one man in his time plays many parts...."

What struck me, after decades of being taught to the contrary, was the realization that just because someone is an intuitive, a healer, a doctor, a professional, or an authority figure does not mean that they live a "holier" or easier life, or are a "better" person, or who ought to be revered. No, they are human. They, too, have, dare I say, jealousies, insecurities, tempers, health issues, chaotic lives, some poor choices to deal with, and so forth. It honestly took me a while to comprehend that, so it was an eye-opener for me. Having realized this, I became less hard on myself, for not being the super self-healer who has totally healed herself lickety split.

I have noticed when I have a negative thought or negative feeling about someone or something, I allow myself to dwell in that melancholy state, to just sit with it, the event, but not for more than overnight. Seriously, why would I want to be in such a state of mind for any length of time? I then work at shifting those negative thoughts and feelings. I do this either through emotional release, asking for guidance from Above, saying prayers, and/or participating in an activity that makes me concentrate on something more productive.

This reminds me of one particular evening.... My husband came home from work, and he could do *nothing* right in my eyes. Finally, he instructed me to go work on myself and release emotions. Here is the amazing part. After releasing two trapped emotions, (just two needed to be released), I asked, for some reason, for the age in which the trapped emotions had occurred. *Oh, my gosh!* That particular day was my Dad's death anniversary. I am pleased to say the remainder of the evening went smoothly.

Here is another way in which I have shifted my being by believing and trusting in the power of energy healing. One weekend, due to family obligations and to keep peace, my husband and I visited a family friend who had a massive streak of narcissism and was a pathological liar. (I'm leaving out all the "good" stuff because I do not wish to give this person's negative energy any more power.) Anyway, before our visit, I prayed the Hawaiian Ho'oponopono prayer, which is a we-are-all-one forgiveness prayer that helps to heal relationships. I prayed it multiple times a day for this person, for my husband, and for myself, until we arrived at our destination. I am humbled to say that this prayer is very powerful. My husband and I spent a wonderful, peaceful holiday weekend with this person.

Because I prefer, and like, the feeling of being happy, I strive for finding the positive in all that is around me. I don't even mind traffic jams. Well, to revise that, I do if I've drunk too much water or café prior to getting into the car! Usually, though, I make a game of traffic jams. I check out the various license plates, car models, makes, and colors, despite the fact they all look similar these days. I look around at the environment. Too often we concentrate so much on driving, or being stuck in traffic, we miss our surroundings. I repeat two mantras: "It is what it is" and "This too shall pass." Then I let it go.

As I progress as an energy healer, I practice various routines – which have changed from time to time since life, of course, is all about change. Before falling asleep at night, I might go through a mental gratitude list, acknowledge and thank Mother Mary, Archangel Michael, my guardian angels; or I might do emotional release healing on myself. What I do is always evolving, as is life.

For me, it is a necessity to take several moments just for me, preferably in the morning, every morning. I call it my quiet time or "Susan

Time." I find that if I do this in the morning, my day seems to go smoother. During my quiet time, I may do emotional release healing on myself, I may balance my chakras, I may pray, or I may sit still and simply clear my mind. Sometime during the day, movement of any sort is a must, such as yoga, simple stretching, bicycling, etc. Every day is different. Nothing is static. And, most importantly, prior to working on a client, I clear myself of any trapped emotions. That way I am totally open, free, and clear as I work with them.

I continue to alter how and what I choose to eat. We only have one body in this lifetime, and we need to treat it with care. Most of us, however, treat our favored possessions with more care than we do our bodies. Observe how you treat your body. There is so much out in the public domain about healthy eating, healthy foods, nutritionals, good water, and exercising. And now, finally, sodas are getting the bad rap I believe they deserve. As for what my husband and I eat, we follow the suggestions of Dr. Joseph Mercola. Check out his website at _www.mercola.com_. We also follow the advice in "That Vitamin Movie" and the video series titled "The Truth About Cancer." Rest assured that, occasionally, we both eat foods that are not healthy but taste oh-so good. Our bodies later let us know our choices were not in our best interest. Yup, we are spiritual beings having a human experience.

I am now more aware of the popular use of negative phrases and idioms, and I urge those around me to cease using such phrases as "It's to die for," "You're killin' me," and "I'm dyin'." These type of phrases are negative vibrations and block positive energy. Remember, words are energy and each word has its unique vibration. Keep what you say positive and uplifting. Even if someone does something stupid, do your best not to berate them. Speak in positive terms. More often than not, the person who made the mistake or error already feels bad enough.

The same awareness applies to speaking of what you do not want. I honestly still struggle with this occasionally because it is so ingrained. However, I know, and I am sure you now know, that this is negative energy and by saying such phrases, only negativity will surface. This was confirmed to me... During the last year of her life, my mother made a point to tell me that she did not want "x, y, or z." Well, what did she get within months? You got that right. She got "x, y, *and* z"! Lesson learned big time. The Universe does not hear "not." So, if you say "I *don't* want ___," the Universe hears "I *want* ___," and that is most likely what you will get.

Society has taught us to identify with our maladies. "My headache...." "My illness...." "My...." However, since we are energy beings having a human experience, these physical symptoms are not truly who we are. We are our heart's energy. The more we take ownership of our symptoms or dis-eases, the more negative energy we give them. Is that what we really want? Our bodies are our earthly vessels. Have you ever been to an open casket memorial and taken a look at the body? The body never looks like the person did while alive. That is, primarily, because their soul, their personal energy, is no longer in that body.

Continuing on the subject of maladies, many people tend to take over-the-counter drugs to ease symptoms such as headaches. I admit that in my younger years, before I "awakened," I took a lot of aspirins to ease headaches, minor aches, and discomforts. What I failed to realize at the time was that I was probably dehydrated, and dehydration can be the primary cause of numerous symptoms. Yes, dehydrated. I believe that too many people are unaware that dehydration is one of the largest killers and causes of dis-ease. As F. Batmanghelidj, M.D., states, "Chronic cellular dehydration painfully and prematurely kills. Its initial outward manifestations have until now been labeled as diseases of unknown origin."[31] The more I have done research on this, the more I am flabbergasted at the simplicity of it all.

I will admit there were times when I doubted all this metaphysical energy healing stuff and wondered if it was all a "pile of crock." There were, and are, times I expect *immediate* obvious results, but they do not occur. At least I am not aware of a shift, even though a shift has taken place. Eventually, I remember it is all in *kairos* time, not *chronos* time. I also remember all the times I have literally healed myself by living in gratitude, by releasing trapped emotions, by trusting in God, and by not believing in the "almighty" power of modern-day, synthetic pharmaceuticals (thus saving my body from their unnecessary side effects). What would this body be like, and what would my emotional state of being be like, if I did not have the healing tools I have developed over the years? I fear this body and mind would not be as healthy. I have such *gratitude* for having "awakened."

As a result of my "awakening," it has become a way of life to do emotional release healing, or even some other modality of energy healing, on a regular basis. It is wellness maintenance, just like brushing one's teeth, cleaning out the lint filter after every use of the clothes dryer, or changing the oil and oil filter of one's car. Regular maintenance of anything keeps it operating efficiently. Regularly releasing trapped emotions, keeps them from getting stuck, (basically upgrading our energetic vibration), thus preventing or eliminating symptoms, or worse yet, dis-ease.

At various times during my spiritual, energetic, metaphysical growth, I have had numerous "ah-ha" moments about my parents and relatives. I realized – whether or not I agreed with how they raised me, with the beliefs they held, or with how they lived their lives – they were doing the best they knew how. They were most likely living their lives in the same way or in a similar way to how their parents raised them. Traditions and customs ruled the day. We are the product of our parents and extended families, and it is up to each of us to decide if this is how we wish to carry on the rest of our life. In one particular "ah-ha" moment, I forgave several relatives for slights I believed they had personally directed at me, but had not. This perceived error was what The LifeLine Technique® calls a lens of misperception. Does it help that they have all passed? *Don't know.* At any rate, I did forgive them all. And just like that, I felt so much more at peace. I forgave them. And I forgave myself.

A gradual shift occurred as it began to register in my brain and heart that we are all children of God. Everyone is someone's child, mother, father, sister, or brother. If anything, we are created to love someone – everyone. No matter their earthly age or position in life, deep down inside, they are just a young child wanting to be loved. As I accept that thought, I am better able to view others with compassion – even if they are treating me or those around them with disregard. Everyone is dealing with their own private angst and most likely are unable to express their deepest emotions (subconscious trapped emotions), and thus are acting out their frustrations and anger. Having said this, mind you, I also say I do not have to like them; I just love them for being a child of God.

This brings to mind a tragic event that was a learning experience for me. I was briefly acquainted with a woman, I'll call Rosie, who I believe came into my life just to teach me the following spiritual life lesson. Rosie and I were both numb and in disbelief because the husband of a woman we both knew was targeted and shot dead while volunteering for a work assignment. As I was going on about how awful the circumstances of this man's death were, Rosie calmly informed me that we must not forget the killer and his family members who were also victims. *Seriously?* Yes, it is a Universal truth. Really and truly. There was no way for us to know what was going on in this man's mind and heart for him to have committed such a heinous act. In order for us to heal our hearts, we had to forgive this man. What an eye-opener and "ah-ha" moment for me.

To paraphrase Dr. Darren R. Weissman, it would be beneficial if we could remember that we do not perceive the truth. We perceive, instead, what we believe. And what we believe is what we've been taught.[32] How's that for a concept? The challenge for many of us is that what we've been taught may not be the truth, let alone our truth or Universal truth.

Alan Cohen wrote about his mother telling him about a "tush cold" in *A Deep Breath of Life*.[33] She instructed him to never flush the toilet while he was sitting on it, otherwise, he would catch a tush cold. One day, as an adult, when he did flush the toilet while he was sitting on it, he discovered that nothing happened. No tush cold. Only then did he realize he did not even know what a tush cold was. He also began to wonder what else he had been taught as truth that was actually an old wives' tale. So, our parents raised us the way they were taught. Knowing this, kind of puts life into perspective, doesn't it?

I've learned to strive for excellence rather than perfection. For years I perceived I was raised for perfection, which put a lot of self-pressure on me. No one can be "perfect," yet anyone can achieve excellence through work and determination. Just knowing this has made life flow easier. *Gratitude.*

As a result of attending a spiritual retreat, which happened to be out of the country, I now realize, from my core, that there is so much more "out there" energy-wise than we humans can even begin to comprehend. Take the most awesome energy healer on the planet, and their abilities are merely a hint of what God/Universe offers. I returned home humbled and in awe.

As spiritual beings having a human experience, we are all, in essence, pure love and all connected. Any actions not based on love are a result of not acknowledging this Universal truth within ourselves. The Universal Law of Free Will allows for us to make our own choices. As we make the choice to release negative trapped emotions, we allow ourselves to move closer back to our essence of pure love. This journey may take decades, yet it is so worth the time and effort. Living in gratitude and love frees us to express a random act of kindness with regularity and ease.

I continue on my path. *Ahhhh!* So much more to learn…. All in good time.

Life is good. All is well. And so it is.

8. Final Thoughts

The greatest revolution in our generation is the discovery that human beings, by changing their inner attitudes of their minds, can change the outer aspects of their lives.

~ **William James**

Do not assume that he who seeks to comfort you now, lives untroubled among the simple and quiet words that sometimes do you good. His life may also have much sadness and difficulty that remains far beyond yours. Were it otherwise, he would never have been able to find these words.

~ **Rainer Maria Rilke,** *Letters to a Young Poet*

Just about every developer of an energy healing modality, as well as those who practice a specific modality, will tell you that theirs is the one and only, the best. I can tell you that each modality has its own time and place in one's healing. With some, you are merely present, either sitting or lying down; with others, you are actively involved. All of them are good. Remember, the process is a personal one. So, at first, go with the one or two that resonate with you.

As emotions are released, you will, in time, begin to notice that you have fewer beliefs that limit you and your abilities. You will feel more empowered to express the true you. As this energetic shift occurs, you will be able to see not only yourself but the world around you from a different perspective. For starters, you will find yourself living and expressing more gratitude for even the smallest things in life. As you begin to express more gratitude, it may seem as if you are gradually pulling aside a sheer curtain from your former emotional and physical perspective, allowing more positivity to flow your way. Heck, gratitude (okay…and having faith in *kairos* time) is the key to happiness in the big scheme of life.

"Your intentions create your experiences," says Doreen Virtue in her book, *Healing with the Angels*.[34] In other words, our expectations, beliefs, and thoughts, especially those ingrained in our being, create our experiences, thus our life. That's because our expectations – whether negative or positive – will attract like vibrations.

Do what you can to maintain positive relationships. If you keep company with someone who is always down or focuses on the negative in life (low vibrations), so will you… in time. Therefore, maintain relationships with those who focus on the positives in life (high vibrations). If you keep the high vibration energy flowing, you will prevent negative emotions from getting trapped. Keep in mind the Law of Attraction, which states that like energies attract like energies. Positive thoughts attract more positive thoughts. Therefore, it holds true that negative thoughts attract more negative thoughts.

As you go about your day, observe your thoughts. Consciously shift those thoughts if they are negatively based. It takes practice, perseverance, and patience to see something positive in what you perceive to be a negative. It is challenging to make personal changes when negative thinking or an unhealthy lifestyle is so ingrained in your being. If you would usually make a negative judgment about someone or something, acknowledge it, then do your best to see what is positive. Or, better yet, as the cliché goes, spend time in their shoes. Make a serious attempt to visualize yourself in their position. Stay there for a while. See if you become less judgmental. Pretty soon, thinking in a nonjudgmental manner will become second nature.

Understand that everyone is on their own path, dealing with their own issues, for better or for worse. Simply knowing this concept may help you notice the shift taking place within you – as you find more compassion, more understanding. Do this enough times and you will soon observe more of the positives in life all around you, and, in turn, you will begin to feel better, and your vibration will increase. After all, the more positives you see, the more positives will be received and visa versus. Watch your words and thoughts, especially as you speak with children. Keep love flowing in your words, as challenging as it may be at times. Children absorb all that is around them. In particular, they emotionally and energetically absorb words (even if said in jest), as well as the tone of voice used to convey those words. Believe it or not, children may interpret the meaning differently than you intended. As they grow, their subconscious will begin processing what does not feel right to their lovely souls. Eventually, unprocessed thoughts will manifest as physical symptoms and/or inappropriate behavior, however that may be interpreted. On the other end of the spectrum, if children are surrounded by love, with respectful discipline, boundaries, and encouragement, they will blossom and flourish as human beings, thus spreading that pebble-in-the-water high vibration to all who are near them.

Remember, we all observe life through our personal, and usually subconscious, lens of perception. Whenever two or more people experience the same event, you will find that each one has a slightly different recollection of the event. What I have learned is that one need not take things personally, although, at times, this is easier said than done. I reiterate, it is in our best interest to remember that everyone is on their own path, dealing with their own struggles. So often their actions/words toward us have nothing to do with us.

If you visualize an image long enough, you can actually manifest it, for better or for worse. The car accident I was in is a perfect example. I had always wanted to know how Princess Diana may have felt being in that tragic accident. A couple of years later I experienced a serious accident, albeit not as horrific, but bad enough to total my Saab and to keep me homebound for two weeks. Lesson learned.

The more your vibrational energy increases, the healthier you will become. Why? Because being healthy is a high vibrational state of being, whereas being ill is a low vibrational state of being. By being high vibrational, there are fewer reasons for emotions to get stuck. After all, you are better able to handle whatever life hands you because you are also living in the moment, embracing life.

Being impatient helps no-one, particularly a panicky impatience. Impatience is negative vibration. We all experience times when we feel impatient. Accept the feeling, and the accompanying emotions, realize that all of life occurs in *kairos* time, then do your best to let it go. Allowing life to unfold in its own time actually allows you to flow with life, and that, is positive vibration.

Eventually, as your energy of positivity, thus your vibration, increases, you will notice that those around you with lower vibration will drop away. Lower vibration people may be those who have low self-esteem, who complain a lot, and who literally drain the energy out of those around them. Those who do not share your spiritual or energy-based beliefs will fade from your life. Losing people in this way may be difficult and sad, yet in time you will realize that you are better able to develop spiritually and/or energetically. This new void will be filled as like-minded thinkers find you – or you, them. It is like cleaning your closet. Old stuff needs to come out, to make room for the new. It is bittersweet.

Be kind as often as possible; even strive to be kind all the time. Be that shining light you wish to see in everyone. You never know how powerfully one act of kindness can affect someone. I first heard about this when I worked at a TV station in Sacramento. One of the creative directors always suggested to coworkers to perform one random act of kindness at least once a week. Wow. Years later, in Florida, I was out doing grocery shopping when a massive rainstorm kept shoppers gathered at the exit waiting for the storm to abate. An elderly man in the crowd, without an umbrella, looked apprehensive.

When the rain eased a bit, I instinctively offered to take him to his car, covering his head with my umbrella and carrying his groceries. He was so incredibly grateful my heart was touched and filled with love for him. It was a random act of kindness that meant so much to this man – and I only got a little wet from the rain.

Here is another example of a random act of kindness, of doing or saying something with kindness that can change another person's life. Shortly after getting married, I volunteered at the American Red Cross office on the Air Force base where my husband was stationed. The position required that I drive around base to various squadrons; thus, I had the opportunity to meet a lot of people of all ranks. One was a young enlisted airman. Because I saw him so frequently, we would often chat. I sensed immense leadership potential in him and encouraged him to go to officer training school. I have nothing against enlisted airmen, yet this young airman had something about him I could not put my finger on, one of those *je ne sais quoi* qualities. In hindsight, he had a very high vibration, a positive energy that radiated. Fast forward a few years.... I had just returned from our overseas tour when I ran into this young airman on base while doing return-to-America errands. We recognized each other immediately. With a huge grin on his face, he informed me that he had kept hearing my encouraging voice over the years, and was preparing to leave shortly for officer training school!

I believe when one simply respects everything, and I mean everything – all your possessions, anything that does not belong to you such as driving a car rental, staying in a hotel room, and so forth – it creates positive vibrations. Because we are all one with the Universe, such actions show respect for all and thus of self. It is something to think about....

I am acquainted with a few people who always seem to have a lack of something in their life: lack of a decent running vehicle, lack of money, lack of education. It feels to me they may have a scarcity mentality, almost a woe-is-me mentality, which has to do with a lack of awareness, almost a helplessness, often passed from generation to generation (or even a traumatic event that has them stuck emotionally). Some of it has to do with a lack of self-worth, and lack of an understanding of how to have a healthy relationship with money. When I visit them, they tend to excuse their condition by blaming others, which is definitely a low vibration action. This view has nothing to do with a person's circumstances precipitated by an economic downturn, unexpected medical expenses, or an act of God, such as an earthquake, hurricane, or a fire. It has to do with a person's less than optimal perception of themselves and not acknowledging their own role in creating their circumstances.

Whenever an opportunity presents itself, if your heart sings with joy or you sense urgency in your heart, go with it. Embrace all that it has to offer, and you will be in agreement with your life's path.

Ego. What a tiny yet powerful word. The ego is most often connected to a deeply rooted sense of insecurity, lack of self-worth, and blame. One characteristic of the ego is that it cannot be wrong. After all, when one's ego is right, one feels better, more powerful, no matter what. So many ills in the world are due to massive egos creating greed and power. Just imagine if one could crack the ego enough to open up to the possibilities associated with a basic love of self, humankind, and life in general. If one looks deep into the core of the rebellious, one may find individuals seeking love and approval. Chances are their childhood has been marked by one or more major unprocessed trauma. The challenge is to let those influenced by trauma know they are loved. It is in their best interest to begin to "awaken," to build clarity of vision, to open their hearts enough to allow their energies to flow in a more positive way. Having said all this, I believe that each of us needs the bit of ego defined as self-esteem or self-worth. The other aspect of ego is the not-so-flattering one: the facade of boastfulness and self-importance that condenses down to low self-esteem and low self-worth.

When I lived in Italy, my hairdresser shared with me his philosophy about hair. He said so many of his clients, if not all, fret about their hair, be it too frizzy, too wavy, too straight, too thin, too thick, too whatever. He would tell his clients to embrace what they did not like about their hair or their bodies, and to just emphasize it! Really? Yes! He said to embrace any physical flaw you believe you have and shine with it. Eventually, you will find that you accept yourself so much more fully. What *gratitude* I have that he shared these words of wisdom. I'd like to add that having negative thoughts about your physical flaws only creates an energetic block, and what we are working on here is to keep that positive energy flowing within ourselves.

Every once in a while, I will attempt to use my non-dominant hand, or walk or bicycle in a different direction if I am out exercising. I like to keep the mind alert by doing something out of the ordinary. As I do this, it occasionally reminds me of my mother when she had her massive stroke. About a year prior to her stroke, she broke her right arm badly. She was right-handed and was forced to use her left hand. She practiced a lot. I was *so* proud of her. After all, she was in her late 80s and was an active, can-do lady. Mom was even able to write very well with her left hand. *Amazing.* A year later, almost to the month, Mom experienced her massive debilitating stroke…. It paralyzed her right side. At least she had previously given her brain the opportunity to practice using the left arm for eating and writing. The lesson here is that we never know why certain situations befall us or when they will happen. We just need to embrace them and move forward. Remember, it is not what circumstances befall us that define us; it is how we handle the circumstances.

This is where gratitude comes in. It is in our best interest to be grateful for everything, even if what we are grateful for is difficult to handle. For example, Mom was rapidly recovering and rehabbing from a minor speech stroke in a medical facility when, late one evening, a staff member was passing by her room and saw her collapse. Mom had suffered another stroke, this one debilitating. Many weeks later, by a fluke (or was it?), I met the staff member who witnessed Mom's fall. She answered all my anguished questions and filled me in on all the details. I learned that, after this major stroke, Mom was never alone for any length of time until late into the next evening. I was immensely filled with *gratitude,* knowing Mom was well taken care of during that traumatic first day. Family friends or a medical staff member was with her from the get-go, until she was transported to a different hospital. Even then, the next day, someone she knew was always by her side.

In another example, I saw an interview of a woman who was injured in a terrorist bombing. Although this woman was seriously injured, her comments centered on all the good people around who came to her aid. She was able to find gratitude in the midst of horror! She commented that it was gratitude that made her able to carry on with life and to heal faster, both mentally and physically.

> *The most powerful thing you can do to change the world is to change our own beliefs about the nature of life, people, reality, to something more positive... and begin to act accordingly.*
>
> **~ Shakti Gawain, Creative Visualization**

I always say that one of the ways to learn about someone's temperament, morals, ethics, and level of integrity is to watch how they handle themselves under pressure or in a conflict. Do they cave in with irrational behavior? Do they lash out or blame others? Do they handle themselves with aplomb? Do they help and guide others? By remaining in integrity, they can stay true to themselves and keep the energy flowing freely.

If you are in the dumps, and have felt emotionally drained for quite some time, it can get discouraging. I've been there; done that. Perhaps, there's a purpose for the discouragement: One often needs to learn what they do not want before they can realize what they do want. At times like this, it is in your best interest to continue to find the best in your circumstances. Imagine that you are a newly planted seed. A seed needs time to germinate. Your life circumstances are creating an environment where you are gathering the energy, the knowledge, or the resources to begin the germination process. Remember, the seed is in a dark space, just like you might be. Fret not. This too shall pass. In time, you will find your way, just as the germinated seed will begin to push through the earth toward the light. Once you break free and find your way, you will begin to blossom just as the plant does. Remember, it is all in *kairos* time. But you "gotta" keep finding the blessings all around you and stay grateful for the smallest things life presents. Take nothing for granted.

Again, I reiterate, be grateful. Be grateful for the green lights as you drive, for the parking space in a full lot, for the friendly sales person, for the food you eat, for windshield wipers working on a rainy day, for a car that runs, for shoes that are comfortable, for the first flowers of Spring, for the birds chirping in the morning…. And the list goes on…. You get the idea.

As I look around and observe what is going on in America – and the world – I believe we humans create the problems we have: war, famine, pollution, crime, and so forth. The problems are based on ego and greed, first and foremost, but ignorance, custom and generations of unquestioned family traditions all play a part. We become close-minded to learning new things, even if they will help us in the long run. After all, change can be difficult, especially if it is thrust upon us.

Custom is a powerful force, for better or for worse. In most cases, a populace carries on what they have been taught, even when their societal customs are not in their best interests. I watched "Lessons of the Loess Plateau," a documentary video written, directed, and produced by John D. Liu, a film-maker and ecologist, about a village in China. The people had farmed and cultivated the land so much, just as they had been taught, that they had completely stripped it barren. Nothing grew in the soil anymore. The people were barely surviving. It took years for a group of multinational scientists to come up with a plan to rebuild the fertility of the land. It took a lot of educating, understanding, and patience, on both sides, to make the project come to fruition. Now, the land is once again fertile, and the people are no longer dirt poor (no pun intended). To regain a thriving community, the people had to shift their centuries-deep mindset. When they decided to trust the scientists and allow their minds to shift, they benefited beyond their wildest dreams. The same can also hold true for those of us who choose to shift our mindset and take that sometimes difficult first step toward getting healthy.

Finally, I believe that each and every one of us can benefit from energy healing, no matter our religious beliefs, social status, or level of spirituality. We are all energy beings having a human experience, and as such, we are all fallible in one way or another. None of us are immune or excluded. Imagine if every one of us healed even one of our emotional wounds, how much better we would all feel. There would be less strife, not only within us but in the world.

<u>Keep Energy Flowing</u>

Our goal is to maintain energy flow. It's sometimes difficult when we get caught up rushing from place to place, meeting deadlines, maintaining a busy household, and most likely running on adrenaline. Despite the seeming chaos, we can maintain our positive energy every day. Yes, it is possible. I hope the following guidelines will help shift your perception of the circumstances in your life:

1. Focus on what is positive.
2. Do your best to be in the present moment.
3. Find blessings in every situation.

4. Accept that everyone sees life from a unique and personal perspective, which may not be in sync with yours.
5. Have and express gratitude.

You are that pebble in the pond, so keep that positive vibe flowing. Once you shift your way of thinking about life, your positive thoughts, your positive energy, and your gratitude will begin to positively affect others. And as the ripple extends out, lives will shift, sometimes imperceptibly, but shift they will.

9. Client Stories & Pet Stories

Our prime purpose in this life is to help others. And if you can't help them, at least don't hurt them.

~ Dalai Lama

Client Stories

The following short case histories are additional examples of everyday emotional release healing. They illustrate the variety of ways trapped emotions can manifest as symptoms.

1. Laura came to me with a sore forearm. She said it had been hurting for days. Her husband, a physician, suggested she take an anti-inflammatory. She did so, several hours before she came to see me, but her forearm still hurt. After we released less than a handful of emotions, she stated the discomfort had moved down her arm. Literally, a few moments later, she exclaimed that there was no more discomfort.

2. Dave came to me feeling worthless, rating his feeling at 6 out of 10, with 10 being the worst. After about one hour of releasing emotions, he rated his feeling of worthlessness at "0."

3. Bogdan, a fellow practitioner who lived in another state, called me on my cell phone. He was in agony with a kidney stone. This was not his first go-around with kidney stones, so he decided he'd call to see if I could release whatever emotions were manifesting as this kidney stone. As life would have it, the timing wasn't the best as I was out shopping with my niece

in the early evening. However, while she shopped, I released trapped emotions. I released quite a few emotions, and by the time I called him back, it was well into the evening. The next morning, I received a text full of gratitude and blessings. During the night, he had easily passed the stone.

4. The very first metaphysical fair I worked at, there was a fellow healer who had his booth directly across from me. He instructed his wife, who he said had unresolved issues, to come see me. To the contrary, she emphatically stated she had worked through all her issues. Yet, after releasing more than 10 emotions – she could not relate to any of the emotions or their associated ages – we finally hit the jackpot. She started to connect to the emotions. We released a few more until her body said *basta*: enough. Later during the fair, she rushed up to me and exclaimed that something had surely worked. Her rings were falling off her fingers at the time of day when her fingers normally swelled up. She acted like a totally different person....happier and lighter in attitude. (Years later, we met again at a fair and she was still talking about, and experiencing, the healing she had that night so many years ago.)

5. Leah had an immense fear of the water, specifically the ocean. The challenge was she lived in a beach community. We released a few emotions, most importantly some related to the time, when she was a small child, she witnessed a near drowning in the ocean. Her ego could not comprehend not being afraid of water. Nevertheless, later that week, she sent me a photo by text: a picture of the ocean she had taken as she sat in her car. Getting so close to the water, for her, was a humongous accomplishment. I don't know, however, if she ever walked on the beach or waded in the water.

6. Reuben had been in an auto accident two years prior to coming to see me. He only remembered coming to after his

car hit a tree. During one of our healing sessions, we were able to reconstruct part of the accident and learned that his head had hit the steering wheel. The fact that he was able to remember more of the accident was healing for him.

7. Lexi, a young, single woman, was in her third trimester of pregnancy. She had little life experience and a dysfunctional family background. She asked me to help her get a handle on her life before she gave birth. Emotionally, she was a mess. We were able to meet only a few times before her baby was born, yet, during those few sessions, I witnessed a strong, determined, intelligent person develop. Despite her tender age, she was a wise soul. I was invited to her baby shower, where I was introduced as her life coach. That felt very rewarding, to be introduced as her life coach. Two years later, out of the blue, Lexi called me in desperation. Her two-year-old baby girl was sick. Could I help her? Lexi instinctively knew the illness was emotionally based. When they arrived, I was impressed by what an understanding, devoted, patient, calm and caring mother Lexi had become. I was also impressed by how many subconscious trapped emotions the poor baby was holding on to. They had moved 17 times since the baby was born! I felt compelled a few days later to follow up with Lexi to check on the baby. She was doing fine.

8. Hillary is an artist who had been in a car accident many years ago. The results of the accident left her with back pain. The one time I worked with her we released several emotions. Then, as we were reviewing at the end, I heard what I thought was her pushing her chair back. She exclaimed that the noise was her back popping! It was the first time since the accident that she had gotten any movement out of her spine! Later that day, she informed me that she was now able to see colors more clearly. Obviously, as an artist, that is important for her.

9. Ivy is a healer in her own right. She struggled to find the amount to charge her clients because she believes that what she does, healing wise, is a God-given gift. So, why should she charge someone? Except for one emotion, all emotions released during our session occurred at the age of two. That one emotion had occurred about the same time she decided to do her healing work as a business. We discovered that this emotion was "stubbornness." She then realized she was being stubborn in her ideas about what was appropriate to charge clients, and that thought stemmed from those emotions unprocessed as a two year old!

10. Lauren is a psychic, artist, and all-around awesome human being. She had always heard voices and seen energies, yet she had never been sure about what to do with them. She had what she called an "inner TV" that was always on so she would hear lots of voices all at once. After releasing various emotions and doing energy release work, she no longer heard that inner TV, just the voices that needed to communicate with her.

11. During a presentation, I asked for anyone with a pain to come up, and I would release two emotions. A woman who had had a pain in her neck for almost 30 years readily volunteered. I asked how she would rate the pain on a scale of 0-10, with 10 being the worst. She rated it at a 10. We released two emotions, which she connected with immediately. When I asked how she would now rate her pain, she looked at me like I was crazy. She had no pain! After the presentation, she approached me with tears in her eyes and informed me that, as she sat back down in her seat, she had felt the energetic weight of the pain literally release and move up and out of her body. Thirty years ago she had experienced immense shock and grief, and for 30 years she had been going to doctors and shrinks to help her with the resulting pain. No one could help

her. Most said it was all in her head. Within five minutes, at this presentation, she was what she called "healed." Just like that. Many years later I ran into her and she happily informed me that she was still "healed."

12. Sue was visiting for a few days. The day she planned to leave, she went on an errand. Just when I expected her back, she called, almost unintelligible. She had broadsided a car, and her SUV was totaled. The accident occurred less than five miles from my house so I got there within minutes. Shortly thereafter, the other driver was airlifted. The accident was bad. Even one of the officers was having a challenge with his emotions while managing the traffic. Because Sue had been driving a large SUV, she was more dazed than physically injured, so one of the officers instructed me to take her to the closest hospital and stay with her in the ER. Her body was shaking uncontrollably. Once in the ER, I went into healer mode and began to release trapped emotions related to the accident. Both of us were amazed when, within minutes (as in under 10 minutes), she calmed down and was coherent.

13. Emily, a junior in high school, was good in math, yet she froze up when taking her exams. The night before a final, Emily phoned and asked me to release whatever trapped emotions were keeping her from confidently taking the math exam. The next morning I received a call from Emily. She had taken her exam with ease and had passed it with the highest score she had ever received on a math test that year.

14. Grace, a long-distance client, called and asked me to confirm whether or not she had been hung in a past life. That was about the extent of our conversation. Later, I worked with her remotely, with me being her proxy, and then called her back with what I had learned in the emotional release session. Yes, indeed, she had been hung in a very recent previous life, in

fact, during World War II. I proceeded to tell her the sex, age, and nationality she was in that past life. Then I told her the country in which she was hung and under what circumstances. (All this was done through muscle testing, using "yes" and "no" responses. When I am "in session," I listen to whatever comes into my mind. I believe these thoughts are not my imagination, but God speaking to me.) A few days later, I flew to the city in which she lived because I, fortunately, was going there anyway for a training event. We commenced the first of three sessions. Now, Grace had a raspy voice and drank way too many sodas of all sorts. She would have a humongous soda for breakfast, one for lunch, one in the afternoon, and then a little bit in the evening. Her voice was also amazingly raspy for an active, nonsmoking young woman. Okay, so this first session was a whopper-dilly, if I may say so myself. We released a large number of emotions. She asked me questions about the folks who had hung her. The responses confirmed the concept that we come to this earth in "family" groups, carrying unresolved issues with us from lifetime to lifetime. The men/energy beings who had hung her were the very same men/energy beings with whom she was currently involved in a lawsuit. As we completed the session, I was stunned. Appearing around her neck was a bright red stripe – about the width of a rope! Grace explained that in this lifetime, wearing tops that expose her neck causes her extreme anxiety. As her body began to release and process the work we just did, she took a very long nap. The next day we continued our work. At the end of our session, a stripe, the width of a rope, once again appeared around her neck. This time, however, the stripe was more of a medium pink in color. Our next session was held remotely several days later via the phone. Grace reported two things: there was no stripe on her neck, and her consumption of sodas was down to one a day. I could tell her voice was not as raspy. She was later diagnosed with "strangulation voice," or spasmodic dysphobia, and is currently being treated for it.

Pet Stories

Pets, too, have trapped emotions. I've learned that one of the most common issues pets have to deal with is being weaned from their mothers too early. As a result, the emotions that are most often released include grief, heartache, confusion, and worthlessness.

1. I once worked with a dog that barked incessantly whenever the mailman was in the neighborhood, not just near its house. During that session, I released a lot of emotions, many of which were connected to the dog being taken away from its mother too soon. When I finished, the dog barked only when the mailman was in front of the house. What a relief for the owners! On a side note: When I, as an empath, got to the fourth occurrence of grief, which made up most of the dog's emotions, I began to whimper. For whatever reason, there was something very powerful and meaningful for that dog with that particular emotion. Immediately, and I mean immediately, after releasing that fourth grief, I stopped whimpering. Just like that. I was amazed.

2. A friend rescued a mutt and, after a few weeks, asked me to work with the dog, which I did remotely. Later that day, I went to visit them. As soon as I came into the vestibule, the dog came running up to me and stayed with me for quite some time. This had never occurred before, despite the fact I had been to the house multiple times.

3. Pets can absorb emotions from their owners. Fifi, had started barking a lot, for no apparent reason. It turned out that Fifi absorbed grief from the owner when the owner's mother died several months prior. Fifi had also absorbed the emotion of insecurity from the owner in relation to her job. Once all the unprocessed emotions were released, the dog was significantly quieter and much happier. And so was her owner!

4. A family asked me to work with their two rescue dogs. They were peeing, pooping, and puking all over the inside of the house. I worked with the older of the two dogs, releasing over 40 emotions from that one dog and then stopped. I never did work with the other dog. Although this was when I was still relatively new with the modality I was using, I knew, ego-free, that I was extremely good at what I did. Nevertheless, I contacted the doctor I studied under and inquired what this was all about. He confirmed what I had suspected. The dogs were absorbing emotions from the owners of the house and from each other, as well as experiencing their own trapped emotions. The household was a very dysfunctional home emotionally, with constant negative energy. The dogs had sensed this and were merely reacting to it all.

5. A friend was visiting and told me about her two cats: Oliver, whom she'd had for years, and Max, her new rescue cat. Oliver would have nothing to do with the new addition to the family. After releasing several emotions from Oliver, my friend and I continued visiting. Keep in mind, this was all done long distance. My friend was with me; the cats were in another city. A couple of days later, my friend called to say that Oliver was now interacting with Max. In fact, the two now seemed to be good friends.

10. My Story

Our story isn't for us in the first place. It never was. It's for others, and those others need you to own it and share it.

~ Joy McMillan

My interest in energy healing kicked into high gear when I attended, many years ago, a metaphysical fair at a conference center, one mile from my home. I was in a blazé, yet curious, mood about the fair.

The first person I saw when I walked in was a woman whose booth/ space was tucked into the alcove behind the open door. She was also the last person I saw as I exited. However, as soon as I left, I felt compelled to see what she did so I backtracked. To this day, I do not know what drew me to her, nor do I remember what we worked on, but I found myself sitting in her client chair, almost knee to knee in the tiny space. I consider this experience a great example of synchronicity: I was at the right place at the right time, meeting the right person for my greater good. This healer, Alice McCall, used her voice as the healing modality. After chatting for a moment, she began to count down my age (…25, 24, 23…5, 4, 3, 2, 1….) in a soothing voice. Although I was very curious about what she was doing, I was, at the same time, thinking, *This is really weird!*

As we approached the time of my birth in the countdown, I mentioned I wasn't feeling too well, that my stomach was a bit upset. She had a calm response: "That's good." *Say what?* As she continued, we got to seven months *in utero*. I told her I seriously felt like I was going to puke. Her response was again calm: "Excellent." I was baffled. I felt like I was going to puke, and she was enthused? She informed me this was the time frame where the negative emotions were being stored, at least for this session. She did not release any emotions *per se*. She used only her voice to do toning. Her voice went up and down a harmonic scale, sort of. I'm unable to explain it. It just was very different. At the end of the session, to my surprise, I did feel lighter. By the time I got home, I noticed I was standing straighter and felt even lighter. *Wow!* I decided there must be something to this emotional release healing...

What I later learned was that Alice was utilizing Cellular Level Healing with Toning to go straight to the cellular memory of my body and release trapped negative energy to transform my physical health.[35]

As soon as I returned home, I immediately called my mother, Irene, and asked her what was going on when she was seven months pregnant with me. It turns out at that time she learned she was carrying twins. The concrete had just been poured for our house, which my father, Edward, had designed and was building, mostly on his own. So, not only was Mom dealing with whatever life situations she was experiencing at the time, but also she was concerned that the house was going to be too small – even before the concrete foundation had time to cure. She was also dealing with whatever emotions a woman goes through when she learns she is having twins, lives far away from family members, already has a toddler in diapers, and is doing her best to outwardly remain the stoic wife.

> *Great adventures await those who are willing to turn the corner.*
>
> **~ Chinese fortune cookie**

I suppose I was brought up in a wellness home. It started with eating healthy food. Mom was always interested in learning new things. In fact, both Mom and Dad, I believe, were prime examples of thinking "outside the box" by not "keeping up with the Joneses." For instance, we were one of the first owners of a Saab, in our hometown of Ann Arbor, Michigan. Saabs were made in Sweden, with lots of quirky details, and we loved it! [Unfortunately, Saabs are no longer made.]

For several months, we also car-sat for one of Dad's fellow professors. His colleague had an English Morris Minor, another distinctively quirky car. We kids loved that car too, as it was so unusual and smelled of old leather. We referred to it as the "English Morris Putt-Putt Minor," because it would go putt-putt-putting down the street. Dad's main concern when choosing a car was safety. It was a lesson and a way of thinking that became the core of who I am. In fact, I like to say that I learned all my car safety awareness and safe-driving skills from him. He was a brilliantly safe driver and had the eyes of an eagle. One time we were driving back from Chicago in our Saab when suddenly Dad mumbled something, sped ahead, then thanked God. Off in the distance, he had seen a car careening out of control in the opposite direction. He then sped up, realizing that if he didn't, we'd be hit. Sure enough, the careening car smashed into a road railing where we would have been had Dad not sped up. Whew. *Gratitude.*

Dad designed and built our home so it was not a typical spec house. It was unique, modern, and solidly built. When my husband and I married and bought our first home, I was appalled at how poorly the mass-produced house was constructed. A typical American subdivision house, it was cheaply built and merely looked good from the outside. Oh, my gosh. What an eye opener.

Mom got interested in eating healthy foods before it was a "kool" thing to do, and she became a follower of Adelle Davis, the 1960's health food guru. Consequently, we grew up eating healthy food. It was just what Mom served, and for us, it was normal eating. We rarely went out to dinner as a family unless it was a very special occasion. Fast food at the time was only McDonald's, and to the chagrin of us kids, that was a treat we were allowed once a year....if that! Don't get me wrong here. I ate my fair share of sugary foods, starches, and other not so healthy foods. In fact, when I was in college, I needed to take a glucose tolerance test one month prior to going overseas as an exchange student. I pretty much failed the test. Yes, my choices in foods at that time were not typical of how I had been raised. Nevertheless, healthy eating was always in the back of my mind. As a result, when I was an exchange student overseas and went out with my friends, they would drink lots of beer or wine. I'd drink maybe one glass of any liquor and be done for the night. Sodas were never part of my vocabulary, let alone my diet. Ever. As a result, no matter where I traveled, I tended to order water or tea – to the dismay of Italian waiters, Greek waiters, and my fellow travelers.

Mom also practiced yoga – Iyangar yoga, to be precise. In fact, when Iyangar came to the local YMCA when I was a junior in high school, Mom pulled me out of school to be one of his demonstration subjects at a half-day workshop. It just so happened to be the same year that I noticed my spine was becoming significantly crooked, creating a noticeable hump. To our frustration, the orthopedic doctor we consulted said there was nothing we could do about it. He did not even mention surgery. He recommended…get ready for this…no exercising, as that would aggravate the spine. He also recommended that I not look up. Truly, he did. For a while, I used this as an excuse to not do heavy housework. That lasted less than a month. I could not sit still and do nothing, so that "medical advice" was quickly forgotten. Mom had hoped that Iyangar would be able to show me some yoga poses to help ease the scoliosis discomfort. After he assisted me into all sorts of contorted poses, I actually did feel significantly better, straighter, for a few days. I practiced yoga for decades afterwards, taking classes on and off. To this day, I maintain various poses as a benchmark for my flexibility. *Gratitude.*

My brother, Tom, was older by two years and was greatly admired by his younger identical twin sisters - that would be me and my sister, Barbara. Tom developed into an independent thinker. In high school, he instructed me to not be influenced or persuaded by anyone who tried to impress me or others by using "big educated" words in everyday conversation. He taught me that speaking in a way for all folks to understand was more important, and, indicative of a person's sensitivity to the everyday person. To this day, I believe those were words of Universal Truth. *Gratitude.*

While in college, Tom went to Poland under the auspices of a Polish foundation. While there, he met up with some of our Polish cousins. One evening, he ate something that did not agree with his stomach, so much so that he ended up in the emergency room of a hospital. The doctors insisted it was Tom's appendix, but one of our cousins was able to convince the doctors that it might be a serious case of food poisoning. Thankfully, the doctors acquiesced and did not operate. Nevertheless, for all intents and purposes, Tom claims he died that night. He recounted how he saw a white tunnel and at the end of it was our beloved maternal grandfather who had passed earlier that year. Our grandfather instructed him that this was not his time, that he must go back as he had a full life ahead of him and things to accomplish. *Whew. Gratitude.* Tom went on to become a well-respected cancer specialist. *Wow.*

As children, we were encouraged to play outside as much as possible. From grade school through junior high, we rode the bus to school. To catch the bus, we had to walk down a very long, hilly block and cross a relatively busy street. To get home, we had to walk up that same long, hilly block – rain, shine, sleet, snow, whatever the weather. We were never picked up in the car due to inclement weather, so we learned to tough it out as kids. It built fortitude. With this type of upbringing, and with all the traveling in Europe as a young child, as a college student, and ultimately living and working in Europe, this body knows it needs to move; it cannot be a couch potato. Again, movement was instilled in us as kids, and as an adult, I appreciate its value, health-wise. *Gratitude.*

I used to joke that I felt like I was born in a suitcase because we traveled so much as kids. Both Mom and Dad were born and raised in Chicago. Dad became an architect in Chicago and worked for Mies Van Der Rohe, and I soon learned that this was a big deal. Dad took a position teaching at the University of Michigan School of Art and Design, so he moved to Ann Arbor. At that time, Ann Arbor was such a small town it was not even on most maps. Because all our immediate relatives lived in Chicago, we did a lot of traveling between the two cities. This was all done by car, before the Interstate Highway System was completed. Most of the roads were two-laners. Potty breaks were either at a gas station or rest area outhouses. This was not that long ago, yet it seems eons in the past.

As a family, we took many road trips. One significant trip was to the West Coast. Dad attended a convention in Oregon, so he took the entire family. For another convention, we drove east to Washington, D.C. Naturally, we did all the touristy stuff during our trips, on the way out, while there, and on the way back. I believe my desire to travel developed as a result of accompanying Dad on his various national conventions and European sabbaticals. I also believe our travels helped build fortitude, patience, an understanding of differences, and an openness to new experiences. *Gratitude.*

My twin Barbara, and I celebrated our sixth birthday in Europe. It was our first time overseas. My professor Dad took his family on his first European six-month sabbatical.

It was during that trip that I learned an important lesson in food. At a meal one day, I ordered hot tea to drink. I added the usual cream, but when I was about to add a sugar cube, my Dad, who was sitting next to me, gently explained to me that, if I added sugar to my tea, I would get thirstier faster. Right then and there, as a five or six year old, I stopped putting sugar in my hot tea. To this day, I am impressed with the self-discipline I had at that tender age. *Gratitude.*

My siblings and I had a relatively strict upbringing. This included going to Catholic school where we were taught by nuns for nine years. We were raised on hard work, strong ethics (which included writing thank-you notes), obedience, kindness to others, love for family, and respect. We were taught to be respectful of everyone and everything. Here, I must be honest...snakes, spiders, and bugs were not included on the list of things I respected until I was a full-grown adult, and even then, it depended on the size. Being honest was also of the utmost importance. If there is no trust, then what do you have in a relationship?

We were also loved and cherished by our relatives, although, as with any kid, we had unloving thoughts toward parents and relatives at times. In hindsight, I realize how I was raised gave me a solid foundation, and I am ever so appreciative for that. (As a result, I do my best to pay it forward with my brother's children as their auntie – and as godmother to one of them.) Oh, that reminds me...being grateful was instilled in us at an early age, yet it never registered then how basic and important it is for an abundant life. I remember a phrase Mom oftentimes said after dealing with something challenging: "Forward and onward!" Perhaps this was my foundation for never giving up? As I grew in wisdom and years, finding *gratitude* in even the most trying of times has carried me through, and helped me process, deep emotional pain.

When I was 12 years old, the three of us kids attended a boarding school for the fall semester. Dad was on another six-month sabbatical to study church architecture. My parents found an international school in Montreux, Switzerland, for us to attend while they traveled around Europe. I have mixed emotions about this experience, but I can say it helped me mature and become more resilient. We certainly learned to be more independent and realized we could indeed function without being "attached" to our parents. Mind you, I am not saying I did not miss my parents. I missed them a lot, yet due to circumstances, I was able to grow as an individual. Although I was in a structured boarding school, I still was able to make some decisions for myself and to think for myself.

The boarding school experience influenced my spiritual and metaphysical thought processes as the result of me once having a really bad sore throat. *Schwester Brigitte,* Nurse Bridget, whom I really liked, wanted me to stay in bed for a few days. However, this created a conflict for me. On that particular weekend, when I was supposed to be in bed, the hugely anticipated school play was to take place at the hotel down the street. I was NOT going to miss that play. Therefore, I willed myself to get better. I *believed* I could get better. As far as I was concerned, anything was possible. I had a huge *intention* to get better in a matter of days. And I did get well enough to attend the performance, against the better judgment of *Schwester Brigitte.* Although I did not feel super well, I did feel slightly better. At the ripe young age of 12, I realized that the mind played a role in healing the body. Nevertheless, this great concept did not register in my brain at that time as an "ah-ha" moment. Instead, I took getting better as a matter of fact and thought nothing of it, really.

What I also came to believe at the same age is that there is only one God and a "kazillion" man-made religions. While still at the boarding school, I came to the conclusion that, basically, what one needs to do is just be kind to others and treat others the way one wishes to be treated. *Simple.*

A Catholic priest would come once a month for an evening catechism class. One evening I asked the priest a very important question. For us to get to church on Sundays we had to walk or take the infrequent bus, so, on inclement weather days then, would it be okay if we went to the Church of England service instead? That church was located between the boarding school and the Catholic Church. (In fact, it was less than half the distance away.) The Church of England, especially if it is the high Church of England, is similar to the Catholic Church. The priest's response was that we could attend the Church of England only *after* attending the Catholic Church. Say what?! That response kind of defeated the entire purpose of going to the Church of England, which was located significantly closer. In my young mind, I would still be going to church, albeit a slightly different church. I would still be getting God's blessing. That experience stuck with me.

Within months of our returning from Europe, an uncle, the husband of my godmother, died unexpectedly, at the relatively young age of 52. After his funeral, my godmother, whom I adored, told me emphatically that one must remove the following words from their vocabulary: *should have, would have, could have.* What wise advice! Her words have stayed with me and have helped me immensely throughout my life. *Gratitude.*

My very first job, other than babysitting and assisting a neighbor when she hosted one heck of a large dinner party, was working in one the first large discount stores. I worked in the woman's department, folding and stocking garments. It was boring yet arduous work, especially when I had to restock clothes after ungrateful, sloppy, demanding customers. This first experience working in a retail environment proved to be a real eye-opener to the foibles of the public, and people in general. One of my co-workers was a reserved grade school classmate who had earned almost a straight-A average. I had admired her until we worked together on that job. I quickly became disillusioned when I discovered her only topic of conversation was gossip, always condescendingly talking about other people, and no other subject. I was appalled. Dad would drop me off at work and then pick me up at the end of my shift. I can remember telling him on many occasion how I strongly disliked this job. He empathized, yet he lovingly told me this was a good experience, and that it introduced me to the sometimes unpleasantness of the working environment. *Gratitude.*

From the time I was a junior in high school through my freshman year in college, a young doctor and his family lived next door to my parents. The doctor was completing his medical residency. He and his elegant and pragmatic wife had two absolutely adorable young daughters who my twin and I babysat a lot. We also got to know the wife well just by hanging out with her. It was this doctor who, using ice cubes and a sewing needle, pierced our ears one Saturday morning in his kitchen. His daughters were meandering in and out of the kitchen, making us laugh hysterically, despite the pain of the needle going through our frozen ear lobes. A few years after they moved, I learned the couple had divorced. It turned out, even while they were our neighbors, they were unhappily married, despite all outward appearances. I learned a lot from the wife: one never knows what goes on behind closed doors; it is not wise to make assumptions, and it is not wise to judge others. *Gratitude* for her friendship and the lessons she taught me unawares. I am so grateful that we are still in touch, after all these years.

I attended the University of Michigan in Ann Arbor, my home town. As a freshman in college, I took, I kid you not, a course called "Physics for Poets." Now, this brain is not science oriented. It is wired, instead, for practicality, and two things I learned from that class have stayed with me.

1. Beware of commercials and ads that say something to the effect of "4 out of 5 doctors recommend this product." Analyze just who was interviewed. Perhaps the questions were skewed for a specific audience to get the desired results. What if the researchers only spoke with those doctors who promoted the product? Knowing that that information can be skewed in such ways, it is fun to watch commercials, listen to the news, and read advertisements. Taking that one course helped me to see beyond the fluff and recognize that it is all fluff and massive marketing meant to influence our subconscious mind.

2. Always pace yourself. My class was given the assignment to walk up to the observation floor of the bell tower on campus.

There are 8 or 9 stories to the top to the observation deck. We were to record our pace and how long it took to get to the top, as well as record any insights we had as a result of the assignment. I discovered there is no need to start out gung-ho on anything. You will most likely be unnecessarily worn out before the end of the task at hand. Lesson well learned. *Gratitude!*

Also during my freshman year, I took a fascinating class, studying the life and works of Rudolf Steiner. He was an Austrian philosopher, playwright, social reformer, esoteric, scientist, artist, educator, and founder of the Rudolph Steiner and Waldorf schools. In addition, he was the founder of Anthroposophy, the spiritual movement, which as a philosophy, teaches and promotes the importance of a child's creativity and analytical skills. I was very impressed by this man and his works. This class was among a handful of experiences that began to form the idea, in the recesses of my subconscious mind, that there is more to the world than mainstream education, thinking, and living.

My study of Steiner also played a role in my spiritual growth. In his book, *Knowledge of the Higher Worlds and Its Attainment,* Steiner wrote, "If we do not develop within ourselves this deeply rooted feeling that there is something higher than ourselves, we shall never find the strength to evolve to something higher."[36] Wow. One of the concepts I took away from the class was that what we need comes from within, from the inner strength of the mind, not from the outer world. What I was learning really piqued my interest, and I remember underlining almost half the book. Definite *gratitude*, for being able to realize another way of looking at life. I would definitely say that studying Rudolf Steiner had a major influence on my "awakening," even if I wasn't aware of it at the time.

During the second semester of my junior year, I participated in a college exchange program and attended the University of Sheffield in Sheffield, England, where I studied education and was a student teacher for one semester.

During my time as an exchange student, a British classmate actually told me quite bluntly that he was not interested in forming a friendship with me because, at the end of the semester, I would return to America. Oh, my. Although his comment stung, I appreciated his honesty. Yet, it would have been nice to become friends with a fellow student. Instead, I became lifelong friends with my critic teacher, Ann, who supervised my student teaching, and her landlady, who ultimately became my landlady, too.

Being alone a lot, my heart actually ached for my twin. I was not accustomed to feeling the emptiness of being alone. Mind you, I do enjoy being by myself to a degree, but this loneliness was rather intense. On one of many solo trips, in particular, while visiting friends who were living in Oxford, I remember stopping on a small footbridge over a stream, admiring the tranquil sight, and wishing Barbara could be with me, sharing the experience. I suppose this feeling is similar to the loneliness happily married couples feel when they are apart, especially when one of them dies. And I suppose this is a good enough explanation when someone asks me what it is like to be a twin. There is a close, energetic bond between the two of us, at least there is for my twin and me.

On one of my trips to London, I stopped at a sandwich shop to pick up lunch. Standing next to me was a pleasant, older woman who engaged me in conversation. With my curiosity increasing, and her gentle demeanor putting me at ease, I accompanied her to where she worked, the London office of the Theosophical Society. The Theosophical Society "is a worldwide body whose primary objective is Universal Brotherhood without distinction based on the realization that life, and all its diverse forms, human and non-human, is indivisibly One." [37]

The word "theosophical" is Greek and means wisdom of the gods: "theo" meaning "of gods" and "sophia" meaning "wisdom." While there, I had a "reading" with a man who proceeded to tell me about my ancestors and about my personal interests. He was pretty much spot-on! I was amazed. There was *no* way this stranger could have possibly known any of this information, and I certainly had not told the woman anything about me personally when we chatted in the sandwich shop. This was my first experience with someone who was an intuitive.

After my exchange program classes were completed, Barbara came to visit me in England, and, eventually, we would tour "the Continent" [the British term for Europe] together. As I was waiting for my twin to meet me at the Victoria Train Station in London, I had some extra time. I stopped at a beverage kiosk and requested some water with ice. It was very warm in London at the time, and I was thirsty. The woman behind the kiosk counter looked aghast at me when I mentioned ice. She informed me that ice in drinks is an American custom. To quench my thirst, she suggested I drink some hot tea. Hot tea to quench thirst? Seriously? Since I was open to learning new things, I followed her recommendation. To my surprise, she was right and my thirst disappeared! She said that ice in the body puts it into shock and is not good for the immune system. To this day, I use the information she passed along to me. *Gratitude.*

As a student traveler, I lived by two basic mantras: "Seek and you shall find" and "This too shall pass." I have found that these mantras have kept me calmer in times of stress and distress. Lordy, did I ever say them a lot. Using them made whatever the unpleasant situation was at the moment much more bearable. In hindsight, I was practicing *intention, faith,* and *gratitude,* but....you guessed it…. I was unaware of it at the time.

One of my jobs while in college was being a maid at the only elegant hotel in town. For some unfathomable reason, as I was looking for a summer job, I wanted only to be a maid at that hotel. The hotel was situated close to the University rather than downtown. After I had been working for weeks and coming home at the end of each day with all sorts of anecdotes, Dad suggested I consider writing a memoir about my maid experiences. I thought it was a daft idea. In hindsight, oh how I wish I had taken up his suggestion! Some of the anecdotes could have been fodder for standup comics. If I had written that memoir, I would have included this event, which is definitely not humorous, but portrays another aspect of life. One day, I was assigned to clean a particular room for a week. The room smelled heavily of cheap men's cologne and another unidentifiable odor. A couple of days later, I met the guest of that room as he was leaving and I was about to knock on the door. He was a pleasant young man confined to a wheelchair as a result of an accident a couple years prior. He was in town for various doctors' appointments at the nearby University of Michigan Hospital. Because he experienced bladder issues, he attempted to cover up the resulting urine smell with lots of cologne. We had what I would consider to be a wonderful chat. I learned that this man was not only suffering emotionally from his recent physical disability but also from the stares and negative comments tossed his way as he went about his daily life in a wheelchair. I was so touched and heartbroken for him. It put into perspective the smells in his room, and it also put into perspective whatever personal issues I was going through at the time. I immediately felt blessed for my life. *Gratitude.* We kids had been raised to respect everyone. I had shown respect and compassion for this young man, and for that he was grateful and thanked me for my time and kindness. Wow.

At this same hotel was a man who worked as the handyman for housekeeping. This man was a college graduate whose other job was working as an aide at a mental institution in a nearby town. Another maid was working toward her PhD. We were the only college-educated employees in the housekeeping department of the hotel. One day at lunch, the three of us sat down and discussed our jobs and lives. The other maid had experienced a fair amount of prejudice and assumptions from various guests. The general assumption was that maids were uneducated. No one had ever stopped to truly chat with her. Instead, they belittled her for having such a lowly job. Lowly? I think not. If all the housekeepers of a hotel went on strike, the hotel would have to close. Maids are the glue that holds a hotel together. One day, that maid came to work very happy. Not only had she completed her thesis, but she had also accepted a job offer in Chicago and handed in her notice. Shortly thereafter, I moved into another position at the hotel working directly with guests at the front desk.

Oh, on a very side note, since I am sharing my life here, I ended up dating that handyman. Phil had a large, loving heart. In time, I yearned for more adventure in my life and broke up with him. It was awful for us both. There honestly was nothing "wrong" with him, but knowing he was settled and content in Ann Arbor, I had to move on. I had the "travel bug" in my soul. Many years later, I looked up my college roommate, Anne, from when I was dating Phil. Lo and behold. Who did she marry? Phil! Rather than be upset, I truly, from my heart, wished them the best. When I asked my former roommate how this had all come about, she said that after she and her college boyfriend had broken up, she wondered if there were any decent guys available. She then remembered Phil and sought him out because she knew what a great guy he was to me. Two wonderful people had found each other. My life had brought them together. *Gratitude.*

Not long ago, someone asked me how my twin and I broke into the modeling profession. I had to call Barbara and ask her if she remembered. Mom would frequently tell us about when we were toddlers and looked so identical, she was approached by a fellow art professor who worked at the Art and Design school at the University of Michigan. He wanted to know if he could take photos of us and use them in his work or sell the photos to agencies. My Mom was adamant that we not be exposed to the world of fashion until we were much older and had a college degree! She believed kids were to be kids. Period. End of conversation.

Once we were in college, we decided to pursue this avenue of work. We had our fingers "walk" the Yellow Pages, created a list of names and numbers, and then made phone calls. [For the younger generation reading this, the Yellow Pages was a phone book of business phone numbers. Back then, we also used a phone attached to a wall in the house to make the calls]. And that is how we got started. One thing led to another and before we knew it, we had one agent for print and one for runway work. We did a lot of fashion shows, some print work, and a local TV commercial. The only time we had separate jobs was for print work. We decided that whoever answered the phone got the job – unless there was a conflict in scheduling. The agencies just wanted "the twins," one or both.

One afternoon, one of our agents called to inform us that we had been chosen to model for a company in a machinery trade show that would take place in Detroit in just over two months. Naturally, we were pleased. We had never met the men representing this company – they had chosen us from our photos. Days later, the same agent called, distraught and apologetic. Apparently, we had not gotten the job after all. We were all dismayed to say the least. About a week or so after that, the agent called again, a lot more upbeat. Another company at the same trade show had hired us – from our photos. So we worked the show, just being pretty models at their large booth. Here is the point of this story.... As we walked around the trade show during one of our breaks, my twin and I saw the company we had thought we were going to work with – *and* the models who had "taken our place." A wave of *gratitude* came over both of us, for the models were dressed in outfits that made them look, to be polite, rather trashy. The company we represented had us dressed in elegant, flowing gowns, exemplifying class and intelligence. They treated us with immense respect. They liked us so much that when the trade show moved down to Washington, D.C. about a month later, they rehired us, paying for all our expenses. Looking at the big picture of life, God definitely had a plan for us that we, initially, could did not see.

After college graduation, I worked at a restaurant in Ann Arbor as a hostess. My twin worked at the sister restaurant on the other side of the alleyway. Both restaurants were owned by the same primary owner. When we were not hosting at our respective restaurants, Barbara and I would do modeling jobs in the greater Detroit area. We did this for about two years. A New York City (NYC) designer's traveling representative was in Detroit one week, promoting the designer's latest line of clothing. My twin and I were the models for a local TV station's fashion segment, showcasing this designer. As the TV hostess wanted to know where we'd been (she was impressed by us), so, too, did the designer rep who strongly suggested we move to NYC.

The designer rep believed we would have far more opportunities in New York than in Detroit. What to do? Although we were working a lot doing fashion shows and print work, we were ready for a change. So, a few months later, we moved to NYC with only two suitcases each. *Faith.*

Life in NYC had its struggles, yet, there was that word...*gratitude.* Barbara and I both had *gratitude,* even for the littlest things in life. One day, during our search for an apartment, which was a full-time job unto itself, we stopped in an antique shop. In the course of our conversation with the owner, she asked us where we lived. *Oy vey.* We had to answer that we were now staying with a college buddy of mine, in a tiny studio apartment, after being at a women-only hotel for a month. She urged us to contact a friend of hers who owned a realty office. We did. The guy showed us a cozy studio alcove in a three-story walk-up brownstone around the corner from his office, which was in the Upper West Side neighborhood of NYC. Before we committed, we checked out an apartment in a section of Manhattan (NYC) referred to as Hell's Kitchen. Zachary, a classmate I had dated briefly in high school, was now living in NYC and told us he was thinking about taking one of a few available, recently renovated apartments in a building there. We met him at the apartment building.

Lordy. All I remember, as I write this, is that the tub was in the middle of the kitchen. My twin and I declined, went straight back to the realtor guy, and signed a lease. As life would have it, the realtor was also our new landlord. The rent was reasonable, or so we thought. A few months later, we discovered we were in a rent-stabilized building and the landlord was overcharging us. We took him to the rent stabilization court. Needless to say, we did not pay rent for a few months, which brought the ire of the landlord upon us. He told us he thought he was renting to some naïve, young, blondes from the Midwest. Was he sorely surprised! Months later, I ran into Zachary and asked him if he had taken an apartment in that building in Hell's Kitchen. He chuckled and replied that, in hindsight, it would not have been a wise move. I agreed. *Gratitude.*

Barbara and I calculated that if we each worked one modeling gig per month, we could pay our expenses that month. However, if we were to enjoy and embrace living in NYC, we ultimately decided to each find part-time jobs. Barbara waitressed at a well-known midtown restaurant that she soon experienced was a unionized restaurant. I briefly worked for the owner of a small modeling agency who could not use us as models. Even though she got excited because we could "model-walk" in flat shoes – apparently a rare skill – she said we were too tall for her. Really? Anyway, my experience working in the business office of the hotel in Ann Arbor appealed to her, and she put me to work for a month helping her sort out various papers that needed to be filed. It was at this job that I learned Manhattan had more than one zip code. Really. Ann Arbor, at the time, only had one. My gosh did I feel naïve! Another part-time job I accepted was waitressing at a café across the street from where we lived. We knew the owners. One day I popped in to visit and was handed an apron because a waiter had not shown up for work. And that was how I started my one and only job as a waitress. I now have so much more empathy for waitstaff. Barbara and I both were experiencing huge learning curves.

Simply being able to walk from our little studio apartment to Lincoln Center, which was ten long blocks away, resulted in pleasant and free entertainment and filled us with gratitude. Merely going about one's life in the city, one could see, meet, sit near, or even hang out with any number of celebrities, some of whom were big names and media favorites. (I actually got to know a few of them and socialized with them outside of their public persona.) Life was always an adventure in NYC, to be appreciated and placed in one's memory bank. We liked the fact that folks walked everywhere. Great exercise, and for free. My goodness, our first year in New York, we experienced not only a garbage strike, but also a transit strike, all going on at the same time!

As we went about our modeling work, meeting big-name designers, producers, and executives, I came to the realization that these big-wig men and women were just that: men and women, human beings, mere mortals. Just like with actors, actresses, singers, newscasters, or anyone in the public eye, they were no different from any other person – except that they had a famous position in life. It helped put perspective on modeling as a line of work. *Gratitude.*

We endured a ton of rejections during that first year in the "Big Apple" (NYC). For example, one famous photographer we were sent to meet thought we were too exotic looking, so he sent us to one of the huge and famous modeling agencies. The owner of that agency thought we were too all-American, so she sent us to the other huge and famous modeling agency. That owner thought we were too exotic for their agency. Confusing, huh? And so it went – until we were hired as house models for a big-name designer on 7th Avenue. We worked for this designer for only one season. It was an amazing experience to have a clothing line designed using my/our body shape, and especially to see those garments later hanging in a premier clothing store in NYC.

While working for this designer, we were sent to the Island of Mustique in the Grenadines in the Caribbean to do a photo shoot for an elegant travel magazine. The photo shoot included another set of twins. For a particular series of photos, we were forced to sit on a decaying tree limb with either ants or termites crawling all over us and biting us. All four of us squirmed in discomfort. I saw no point in being bit like this, so I politely said something. The photographer retorted that he was not interested in our safety, just the photo. In addition, he told us, in no uncertain terms, that models were not supposed to speak during a shoot, not even if they are being bitten by insects! Not long into the shoot, we were asked to leave. We were shocked. The other twins thought it was because we had too much intelligence. I kid you not. The other models completed the shoot. We also concluded, from talking with them, that we were sent home not only for speaking up about being bitten by the insects, but also because we had refused to sleep with the photographer. Shortly after returning to New York and our house model job in the showroom, the financial adviser to the designer took us out to dinner. He propositioned us, and we politely refused. We were stunned that we were propositioned first by the photographer and then by the financial adviser, both in the same week. How weird was that? When we arrived for work the very next day, we were let go. Yes, we were shocked and upset, yet, there is more to this story...

While we were in Mustique, we met Brian, the man who oversaw the island's one and only hotel. We became professional friends. More on that later.

When the designer job ended, we signed up with a small agency. Through them we met Angelo, a model who was also a flight purser for a now defunct international airline. Angelo was signed with this small agency when he was in America and when he was in London, he was signed with a London agency. So in-between his flying schedule, Angelo kept busy with modeling gigs. He urged us to send out "Zed cards" to his London agent because he believed we would work more overseas where the models were not so typecast. [A Zed card is a photo card about the size of a paperback book, with one's physical attributes and various photo looks. It serves as a business card for models and actors.] Within a fortnight we were invited to join the purser's modeling agency in London. We never did see Angelo again. In hindsight, I consider our meeting to be providential.

After we were accepted by the London agency, I helped Barbara pack down our apartment, found a sublet tenant, and somehow found time to appreciate our parents who were visiting – all while I was still waitressing at the local café. The day we moved, we had a photo gig in the morning. The memorable part of this story is that the art director was Peter, a kid we grew up with! We did not even know he had moved to New York. In fact, he moved to NYC one month after we did. His Dad and our Dad were professor friends from the University of Michigan. In the afternoon of our photo shoot, we did our final packing, and off we went on our night flight to London. It was comforting to have Mom and Dad come with us to the airport to see us off. Happy memories. [In those days, family/friends were able to wait with passengers at their departing gates.] *Gratitude.*

In the past, the London agency had arranged flights and accommodations for their models; however, they had ceased offering that service the previous year, so we were on our own. Where to live? Since we were still in touch with Brian, we phoned him. Lucky for us, he had room for us in his large flat, in this case, a townhouse in a tony section of London. By the grace of God, he allowed us to stay there rent free. All we needed to do was pay for our share of the telephone bill and our food expenses! Granted, his older brother and another man also lived there, both of them part-time residents. They were always gentlemanly to us. Occasionally they would bring home their girlfriends. It all worked out smoothly and respectfully. We lived in Brian's flat for almost a year and were friends for many years afterward. *Gratitude.*

One day, while I was on my way home to the flat, I all but bumped into Diana Spencer, the soon to be Princess Diana. She was absolutely stunning. I was enamored and couldn't wait to tell my twin and flatmates. After that close encounter, I followed her life, but not obsessively.

I had lived in England before as an exchange student, so getting readjusted did not take long. This time, however, I was not a student or a tourist, but a working visitor. Therefore, I had to learn my way around to get from the agency to a go-see in a timely manner. A go-see, sometimes called a "cattle call" – where we were sometimes two of umpteen girls of similar size and shape – was an audition with a potential client. A go-see could take a matter of minutes or it could take an hour. At a go-see, we would meet a photographer or job director who flipped through our portfolios, observed how we model-walked, and what we looked like in person. The agency promoted us as the American twins, so my twin and I did all our jobs together. There were times we would have as many as five or six go-sees a day, *all over* greater London.

We would take the Tube (the subway) from our flat to the agency. Once at our destination stop, we would then walk several blocks to the agency. The first week was amusing. Still operating on a New Yorker's schedule of rush, rush, rush, we would speed past all the pedestrians on their way to work. Eventually, we noticed that we were the only ones walking rapidly, with intent. Everyone was walking at a normal pace, if not strolling. "Ah-ha!" Why were we rushing? No one else was. And, until we realized that, we would arrive at the agency out of breath, only to be greeted with "Mornin', girls! Cuppa tea? Have a seat while we complete your go-see list." *Gratitude* for a different, calmer lifestyle.

A few months into our London experience, our agent called to offer us an opportunity to do a gratis job. After some cajoling on her part, we accepted the unpaid job. No kidding. It was gratis. So why did we do it? It was a promo video for a new-wave British group called Ultravox. We could not pass up this once in a lifetime opportunity.

Just the sheer experience of being in this promo video for the song, "Vienna," was worth it. We were on set for over 12 hours for an end result of a few minutes of video. The scenes we were in totaled less than six seconds. We started late at night and continued until the middle of the next day. What a blast we had, even if it was hurry up and wait for all those hours. You can view the video by going to YouTube - Ultravox Vienna (official video). So kool!

From London we moved to Barcelona, Spain. Barbara and I were the first in our family to travel, let alone live, in Spain. Exciting! I would have to say that Barcelona is one of the most beautiful cities I have ever visited. Granted, I know it has changed a lot since then, but our experiences there are forever etched in my mind. Even the not so great times are part of that wonderful experience. I loved living and working in Barcelona. Toward the end of our three-month stay, I was dreaming in Spanish.

Our only unpleasant experience happened one day when we almost became victims of a scam. We were out and about, more or less sight-seeing, after a go-see with our portfolios in hand, when a guy approached us. Speaking in Spanish, he informed us that we each had something on our shoulders. Sure enough, both of us had what looked like wet sand on our shoulders. We never felt anything nor did we smell anything. Unbeknownst to us, we were about to get scammed. This is how it works. Two guys work together. They find vulnerable people (usually unsuspecting tourists – I never thought myself to be vulnerable as such, but we were tourists for all intents and purposes). One guy somehow gets an unscented muddy type of goop on your shoulder, draws it to your attention, and then escorts you to a nearby large outdoor fountain where your first thought is to get rid of this stuff. Your second thought is that this guy is a good samaritan. As you place your belongings on a bench and turn to wash off the goop, his accomplice comes by and steals your purse and anything of value that you've placed on the bench – all gone in an instant. However, in our case, they did not count on me turning around and noticing our purses missing. Spontaneously, I cussed in Italian, using the one cuss word an English-Italian photographer in New York had taught me, and took off running after the guy. He eventually turned to face me and – I kid you not – he *stooped* down and gently placed our purses on the ground before he again took off running. Thank you, God! *Gratitude* for having all our stuff intact! What made me turn around to check on our stuff? Instinct? Intuition? Don't know. About a week later, we met a retired, widowed American woman who had fallen victim to the same scam. She was not as fortunate – they took all her money and her train tickets. All alone, she was on her "trip of a lifetime" and, literally, had her life savings stolen. We escorted her to the American Embassy and stayed with her until the embassy folks could assist her. Oh my.

Eventually, it was time to move on to another country. Though it was really tough to leave our beloved booking agent, and especially tough to leave Barcelona, our next adventure took us to Zurich, Switzerland. Who knew Zurich was a center for the fashion industry? But we worked a lot. However, before the Swiss agency would earnestly promote us, we had to pay a chunk of change for work permits! Our first few paychecks went straight to pay for them. Very strict indeed. Unfortunately, after only two months in Zurich, we got word that the guy who sublet our New York apartment had left earlier than expected, and without notice. We skedaddled back to America to save our apartment. If our landlord found out, he could terminate our lease, and we did not want that.

By coincidence, about this time, Barbara was getting disillusioned with modeling. She wanted to quit, but I was not yet ready to end this career. In truth, she had been ready to quit when we left Barcelona. For at least a year we had been living a transient life, meeting mostly wonderful people, only to leave them for the next adventure. Saying so many goodbyes takes its toll on one's heart. However, for me, the scoliosis was getting to a point where I could no longer hide it by standing a certain way. It was causing more and more discomfort. Willing or not, my body was forcing me to change careers.

With heavy hearts we returned to America, a move which was extremely rough on both of us. There was something about the European lifestyle Barbara and I both loved. There seemed to be a greater respect for life. There was less useless violence. They ate real food and less processed food. They took time to enjoy their meals and found no reason to rush through them as Americans tend to do. Each time we had to reacclimate to American culture, it got harder and harder.

I will admit I was depressed for weeks after we returned to New York City. I will never forget this. Once we got over jet lag, my twin scoured the newspaper, went out one day, and came back with a job. She had been hired to work in a big-name woman designer's showroom on Seventh Avenue.

What did I do? I stayed in our apartment – jammies on, curtains closed, watching TV. Boy, oh boy, was I depressed. Then one day, as I watched the local news on TV, a reporter interviewed a young woman with a significant disability. Due to bureaucratic budget cuts, she was about to lose her subsidized and specially outfitted apartment and would have to move back in with her parents. They still lived in the slummy projects in a crime-ridden area of the city. Distraught, she elaborated on her plight. By the time the story was finished, I was sobbing. Who the heck was I to feel sorry for myself?! The next day I went out and found a job.

I managed the showroom of a men's sweater line of a Philadelphia-based company. The showroom, along with two other showrooms, was located in a suite in the Empire State Building. I was the only young person in the suite. I was also the only non-native New Yorker in the suite. I was thrilled to have this job.... I was working in the Empire State Building!

Thankfully, my boss and I had a good relationship because, somewhere around the fourth month of employment, I called him at home late one Sunday afternoon to ask a favor. (Lordy, just thinking about this, I chuckle at the audacity of it all.) A guy I was dating worked for ABC Sports and was in Kentucky for one of the horse races. He invited me to join him for a long weekend prior to the race. Even though I couldn't stay for the race, I accepted the invite. I told my boss I'd be flying back on Monday and would return to work on Tuesday. What *chutzpah!* The traveling bug had "attacked," and I could not resist. My boss and I made a deal that allowed me to stay for the long weekend. Gratefully, all was well when I returned. However, he did instruct me to never, ever, do that again. After working diligently with my boss for about two years, I realized I was going nowhere within the company. As a result, I began interviewing during my lunch hours.

I struggled over which direction to go for my next job. Having worked as a fashion model in both America and in Europe, and now working in the wholesale fashion industry, I began to wonder just how this sort of work helps mankind. I realized that, as much as I was involved and into fashion, I felt it was still all fluff in the big scheme of life. Nevertheless, since I had already spent so much time in front of cameras and in TV studios, it seemed to me the next logical step was to branch out into television. Despite this newly desired direction, I continued to apply at various fashion houses, even at new start-up companies for strictly mail-order fashion lines. Mail-order fashion catalogues were a novel idea at the time. Writing this now, I realize how far the fashion industry has come, even in my lifetime. Wow.

I interviewed for a position as a designer's representative in a well-known department store. My job would be to merchandise that designer's collection. To my delight, I was called back for a second interview. When I did not get the job, I was devastated. The reason given for not hiring me was that I did not have enough experience. Granted, I did not have a merchandising degree, but I did have a few years of merchandising experience in a wholesale showroom and retail experiences in Ann Arbor. Thinking back to the very first month I spent in NYC, fresh from Ann Arbor, I saw a "Help Wanted" sign in the window of a woman's clothing boutique on Madison Avenue and applied for the position. The owner informed me that I had no NYC references; therefore, she would not even consider hiring me! *Really?!* [As a general complaint about interviewing for any type of job, how can one get experience if one is not given the opportunity to learn and then prove themselves? It becomes a catch-22.]

I did one temp job for a woman who was attempting to start up a psychic newsprint magazine. She hired me to put my face on the premier cover. (That may have been the one and only issue; I do not recall ever seeing any subsequent copies.) The photo, computer generated in odd colors, was mostly pixilated. I did not care for it at all. Be that as it may, in lieu of cash payment, she asked her friend, an intuitive/psychic reader, to do a reading for me. Seriously. He lived close to the Empire State Building where I worked, so I met with him during one of my lunch hours, as appointed. To my dismay, he had a major hangover from a night of partying. Nevertheless, he insisted on doing the reading, so I agreed to stay. In a nutshell, he told me that he saw me at a desk surrounded by lots of papers and bright lights. Interesting. Later, as I was thinking about what he had said, I remembered another reading I'd had many months prior. The sister of a make-up artist I had worked with on a job had done a card reading and had pretty much said the same thing.

Hhmmm.... I put the readings in the back of my mind and forgot about them both.

Summertime in Manhattan provided a plethora of outdoor markets and street fairs. At one such street fair in our neighborhood, Barbara and I enjoyed strolling around, calling out to each other whenever we found something of interest. On this particular day, a man approached me by name and started chatting. I had no idea who he was, but he had apparently overheard us calling out to each other and saw that as a great opportunity to meet one of us. (Because of that encounter, Barbara and I began to refer to each other using a generic foreign language word.) He said he was some local political official and invited me to accompany him to a Lena Horne concert that week. His name and face did look vaguely familiar, so I cautiously accepted. The evening arrived and a grand vehicle, not quite a limousine, arrived at my apartment building. The driver greeted me at the door saying that the man was, at the last minute, called away for official duties and was unable to attend the performance. Would I accept his apologies and his gift? The gift was Shirley MacLaine's book, *Out on a Limb*. I graciously accepted. He also said that my twin could accompany me as there was now an extra ticket. So, Barbara hurriedly got ready, the driver escorted us to the car, and off we went. Poshy and elegant. The Lena Horne performance was phenomenal, and our seats were in the second row. Oh, were we impressed with the entire evening, especially when Lena Horne would look at us and smile. As for *Out on a Limb*, that book was a keeper. For me, it was an eye-opener to the spiritual and metaphysical way of thinking. *Gratitude.*

Yet another step to my "awakening" occurred one weekend evening. I called my brother, Tom, a doctor, about some medication I had been prescribed. I was experiencing some side effects from the medication and needed his advice right away. He instructed me to immediately stop taking the pharmaceutical. He said the risk of kidney damage far outweighed the reason for taking the drug. That was one more eye-opener. Why would another doctor, especially one I respected, prescribe a drug that was unhealthy for me? And that was the beginning of me questioning anything that was prescribed for me.

As life would have it, I dated someone from ABC and someone from NBC, both in the sports departments. I chose not to use their connections, so I went to CBS and applied for a job. Almost immediately, I had my first interview, then a second one. When I returned to my office in the Empire State Building after the second interview, I instinctively began to clean out the drawers of my desk. Within a couple of hours, I got the anticipated call. My two-week notice was received with much protest from my boss, but I trusted my instinct. I had a knowingness. Initially, I was taking a slight cut in pay because the position was a maternity leave fill-in position with the possibility of staying on. Yet, I had no hesitation in accepting the job. I was not looking back.

I worked at CBS-TV for four glorious years. I had fantastic bosses and feel blessed to have been their employee. Initially, I worked at the Broadcast Center, where many of the studios and the technology center were located. It is not an exaggeration to say that I regularly thanked God for my job at CBS. I loved my job.

About three years after I started working at CBS, the network was about to be bought by a large corporation. Yet, in the midst of the tensions within CBS, I went on a month-long medical leave to have my spine straightened. It was an incredibly invasive surgery that was done at a hospital in New Jersey. Because scoliosis surgery is usually done during childhood, I was placed on the children's ward of the orthopedic unit. To my surprise, one of the CBS managers had a teenage daughter who was also having scoliosis surgery. Her room was right down the hall from mine, and we shared the same surgeon. The manager and I kept in touch outside of work for a few years after that. Nice. It took more than a year to fully recover from the surgery. What I went through to have a straighter spine! Lordy. But it was worth it.

When I returned to work, I was reassigned to Black Rock, the corporate headquarters, as the result of a major reshuffling of jobs and positions. Now owned by a massive corporation, CBS lost its family feel. I was one of the lucky ones to keep my job, albeit, a slightly different position in a different building. I was still ever so grateful and excited to be working at CBS; however, deep down inside, I knew I was not "meant" to be a corporate employee like this.

While at Black Rock, on pleasant days, I would eat lunch in my office and then walk to St. Patrick's Cathedral and sit in the back. Having this inner quiet time – while masses were being said, while tourists were milling about, and tour guides were giving their spiel – was my form of meditating.

One summer weekend, my twin and I were in the Hamptons, at the summer residence of her boyfriend, when we received a visitor. Neil, a childhood friend, was in NYC for a conference and had decided to look us up. After college Neil had moved to Sacramento, California. He invited us out to visit, saying he had an extra car and plenty of room for visitors.

Neil's words resonated with me. It took a while, almost a year, for me to adjust to the thought of moving to Sacramento, but once I did, everything fell into place. I decided to leave New York City after Easter because I loved Easter in the city, especially at St. Patrick's Cathedral. I had an *intention*. I knew instinctively that this was what I was meant to do: leave New York City and move to California. My brother drove out from a Detroit suburb to assist me in my move, and we drove back to Ann Arbor, our hometown, in a fully packed car. We drove all day, arriving at sunset. To me, that was such a gift – the sunset. *Gratitude!* A completely new life lay ahead of me, and I was ready. I was now officially on my latest adventure.

On a side note, in October, a few months after returning to work after the scoliosis surgery, I took a trip to Sacramento to visit Neil and to check out the job environment. Just before this trip, my Uncle Ray, an uncle dear to my heart, had suffered a debilitating stroke while visiting his daughter, Nancy, in California. I made a side trip to visit him. I took one heartfelt, eye-to-eye look at him and instinctively knew he was not going to live much longer. For the Thanksgiving holiday, I flew home to Ann Arbor. On Thanksgiving morning, I awoke at 3 a.m. and said out loud, "Crap, I've got nothing to wear to his funeral." I then went back to sleep. When I woke up later, the experience was more like a dream and was not forefront in my mind. Midday, while visiting my brother, a California phone operator called him at home. (As a doctor he had an unlisted number). On the line was Nancy informing us that her dad had died at midnight. "Ah-ha!" So my uncle had indeed "come" to me to tell me he had died; I consider myself ever so blessed. I felt we had indeed connected in the hospital on a soul level, as well as a physical discomfort level, having recently gotten out of the hospital myself. Our situations were different, yet similar in an odd way. Uncle Ray lived in Chicago so his body was flown there for burial. Our family drove from Ann Arbor to Chicago for the funeral. Because I had planned clothes only for Thanksgiving at home, I had to scramble to find funeral attire, hence the half-asleep comment. It was a difficult funeral for me. Besides the fact he was a dear uncle, I was still what I considered geeked out, with an odd stance, being unable to cry or laugh due to the pain from my surgery.

When I finally moved to Sacramento, I stayed with Neil for a month until I found a place of my own and got settled. Soon after I moved to Sacramento, I met a wonderful man. I met Art at church, the first time I attended mass in Sacramento. He was newly divorced and struggling with an ex-wife who was crazy, literally. One time he and I were out walking, discussing some issues he was experiencing with her. What came out of my mouth sounded like an experienced shrink who was channeling some wise person. It was so profound that both of us stopped in our tracks and exclaimed about how profound my advice was. I knew then that God was speaking through me. And this was years before I had even shifted how I thought about life.

A few weeks after I met him, my birthday week rolled around. That week I got teary-eyed easily. The day before my birthday, he and I were talking about my birthday, and I broke down into a big-time crying spell. Curious as to why I was so upset, he gently began asking probing questions. It did not take long. Right after the second question, we both had an "ah-ha" moment: This year was the first year in almost forever that I was not celebrating my birthday with my twin. Once I acknowledged the source of the tears, I shed no more about that subject. Art and I had, unbeknownst to us, released trapped emotions. At that time, I just thought that we had figured out the source of the emotions. But we had done much more: We had released them. Little did I realize that we were doing emotional release healing. What a gift. *Gratitude.*

Art also guided me in realizing some of my shortcomings or insecurities. During the time we dated, I believe I blossomed as a result of knowing him. Art taught me a lot about loving and expanding one's creativity. In addition, with his encouragement, I began to draw and to be creative with everything I did. What helped, too, was that Art was an artist himself, a wonderful, free-flowing watercolorist.

After two years of dating and a fulfilling relationship, I broke up with him. I was devastated, yet I knew in my heart that this was the right thing to do. I was breaking up with my best-est friend. There were some issues he needed to resolve, and, I instinctually knew there was someone else for me. *Faith and trust.*

As a newly relocated person from New York, finding work in the television or radio industry was challenging, challenging beyond my comprehension. To pay my bills, I took various jobs, learning all along the way. One such job was working in a little boutique shop in Old Sacramento. During my lunch hour I would stroll around Old Sacramento. One day I met a woman who worked several shops down from the boutique. She was a lot of fun, and we became friends. Jeannie was older, had an infectious laugh, and had very short white hair that she spiked. I liked that she spiked her hair. It showed she had spunk, and spunk she had. By day, she worked as the cashier at the shop, but, in her private life, she was a phenomenal psychic. We had many an adventure together. I have such *gratitude* for having known her. She taught me so much and introduced me to the spiritual and metaphysical aspects of life. She liked the books *Celestine Prophecy* by James Redfield and *Journey of Souls* by Michael Newton. She, of course, made sure I read both of them, and those two books definitely helped me on my path to "awakening." A few years later, perhaps five, God took Jeannie, suddenly. There has been a huge void in my heart ever since, and I miss her oh so much, even now. The only way I can take comfort is to selfishly create a story that God knew that the lessons I learned from her would prepare me to carry on with my path. I swear she was with me as I took a difficult national teachers' exam – which I passed, thank you very much, even though some experienced teachers had to take it multiple times. The woman who sat next to me during that exam seemed to embody Jeannie, and even had a similar name! The woman unknowingly gave me comfort and confidence.

Almost six months passed before I found a job in television. No one could fathom why I would willingly leave the number one TV market and move to a lower market. To them, it was a step down. For me, it was a change in lifestyle: a welcome change and, in my head, a healthy one and one with better winter weather. At wit's end, I contacted an acquaintance at CBS who had recently moved from San Francisco to NYC. I asked him if he had any suggestions for me. I called all his referrals. Every one of them said they were actually downsizing and had nothing to offer. Only one person asked for my resume, and he said he would pass it along to his girlfriend who was an assistant manager at an independent television station in San Francisco. Eventually, I was hired at that station. *Gratitude.* I stayed there for one year, one month, and two days. How do I know the exact time frame? Read on.

I became known at the TV station for walking all over the place. In fact, during many lunch hours, I would eat at my desk while others were away. Then, I would change shoes and go walking up and down the hills of San Francisco. By the time I returned, my legs would feel like Jello, and I was happy. Because I worked on the top floor of a four-story building, I was also known for walking those four flights of stairs. Once in a while, I took the elevator, but it was on rare occasions. On one such rare occasion, at 5 p.m., I received a phone call from a co-worker on a lower floor. She finally had ready the work I had patiently been waiting for all day long. So, off I went to collect it. The elevator door was open and, without even thinking, I walked in and pressed the button for the second floor. No sooner had the doors closed than the elevator began to shake violently. Violently. My mind raced to images of the elevator crashing to the bottom and me dying. Multiple expletives came out of my mouth. After what seemed like an eternity, the elevator, still shaking, arrived at my destination. The door opened just enough for me to squeeze through sideways. Once I was safely out, the shaking stopped, as did the power in the building. *Gratitude.* A trusted co-worker from another department came rushing out of the break room exclaiming, "For this building to shake this much, this must be a big one!" That was all I needed to hear. No longer was I fearful. *Gratitude.* I was now living and experiencing a massive earthquake. Adventure!

The earthquake was the Loma Prieta earthquake, the magnitude 6.9 earthquake of 1989. I was unable to get to where I lived in Alameda because a section of the Bay Bridge had collapsed. So I stayed at a co-worker's apartment in San Francisco. What an adventure Sharon and I had. First we escorted another co-worker home. Then we checked in on Sharon's elderly mom who was dressed and ready to go, with her white gloves on, to the opera. Her mother was disappointed that the opera would not be performing that evening. Sharon and I eventually made our way to her apartment. Along the way, we marveled at how easily strangers were working together to help out their fellow man.

The previous Christmas, my brother had given me a tiny flashlight, which I kept in my purse. Lucky for Sharon and me! By the time we finally arrived at her apartment building, it was dusk. With no street lights on, her section of town was blacked out. My little flashlight became a lifesaver of sorts. It lit the way up the three flights of stairs and down the long hall to her place and guided us in and around her apartment until we could get other flashlights working. We dared not light any candles at this point. We did not smell gas, but we chose not to take a chance. On our way to her place, we had seen in the distance plumes of smoke marked by eruptions of huge flames, the result of a gas main break in the Marina district. Yes, the flashlight was a blessing. *Gratitude.*

A couple of days later, we returned to work. The elevator was still stuck in the same partially open position as when I squeezed out of it during the earthquake. After that first day back, immediate work completed, I was cleared to return to Sacramento, where I spent weekends, to be with Art and my twin, Barbara, who had very recently moved there. (She happened to be in Candlestick Park for the World Series game, so she, too, had had an intense earthquake experience.) By this time, BART (the Bay Area Rapid Transit) was back up and operational, but before I could return to Sacramento, I needed to get to my car. I had parked it near the Oakland West BART station, just outside a warehouse. By the grace of God, when I was with Sharon checking in on her mom, I was able to contact a person who worked at the warehouse and asked them to check on the condition of my car – a Saab, of course. Phone service was definitely intermittent at the time, so the fact that I was able to reach someone, someone who was kind and who actually called me back, was a blessing. *Immense gratitude.* My car was fine. Thank you, God. So now I was able to begin the trek to my apartment in Alameda. When I arrived, I was surprised to find that nothing was affected. *Gratitude.* Then I drove, still a bit shook up, to Sacramento. At the start of my trip, a rock or something came out of nowhere and cracked the windshield. I yelled at God, "Enough is enough! Please do not test me again!" Thankfully, He listened and complied. This was on a Friday. I was stoic until Sunday when I broke down in church.

I returned to work Monday and by the end of the week, turned in my resignation – which was rejected. So we compromised, and I remained for another month and two days.

When I returned to Sacramento, I assisted a girlfriend at her physical therapy clinic. I did that until I found work as a substitute teacher. Eventually I got back into television work. I contacted a former interviewer, Debbie, whom I had stayed in touch with over the years. She was now working at a different TV station, where she found a position for me, and even became my immediate boss. All the while I worked at this TV station, I applied for work elsewhere to no avail. My self-worth suffered, and I felt stuck. I found very little for which to be grateful, other than having a job. I knew working in the business office was not where I was to be. At least I did a long stint in the newsroom and loved the action. I found it interesting that of all the people I had interviewed with over the years, Debbie was the only one I had wished to remain in contact with, and she with me. When I had first interviewed with her, shortly after arriving in Sacramento, her rejection letter had included a handwritten note to keep in touch. So I had. There are no coincidences.

Eventually, a local salesman for the TV station moved to Monterey, California, and became the assistant general manager at a TV station there. He recruited Debbie to manage the business office. Not long afterwards, Debbie recruited me to work there, too, this time as an assistant to the local sales manager. I jumped at the chance for a new opportunity. Some of my responsibilities included selling advertising time to paid programs during odd hours of the day, mostly the wee hours of the morning. I became phone friends with so many of my contacts. My first year there was full of learning curves and adventures, and, practically every weekend, I drove the three hours back up to Sacramento, in my Saab. I loved the drive!

In general, my family's social circle in our middle-class neighborhood was connected in one way or another with the University of Michigan, such as artists or professors. Other neighbors were either teachers, worked in the legal profession, worked for the city, were store owners, or worked at Ford Motor Company. When I moved to NYC, I met mostly actors, actresses, fashion designers, lawyers, TV directors, or financial folks. I never gave it a thought. Then I moved to Sacramento. My perception of my world shifted dramatically. For the first time, I met those who were cattle ranchers, fruit growers, nut growers, rodeo riders, and cowboys. I knew our food came from Mother Earth, and we even had a little garden when we were growing up. Yet, I never contemplated actual fields (other than corn or blueberry bushes) of artichokes, or avocado trees, or nut trees. Even rice fields were regularly burned in the outskirts of Sacramento. Oh, and then there were all the military bases in and near Sacramento. Until moving to Sacramento, I thought I was a well-rounded person, but oh no. I had a lot to learn about life.

My second year in Monterey, I met Tony in the laundry room of our apartment complex. He was in Monterey to learn proper Italian at the Defense Language Institute. He was younger, shorter, and moving in four months. I was not interested. Yet, there was something different about him. Meeting him gave me a new purpose. He brightened my life. One weekend, Tony and I were on a very platonic date to Yosemite. It was there an inner voice told me, as I quivered, that he was the man I was to marry. I've heard married folks say many times that when you know, you know. Now I get it.

Four months later, Tony moved to Italy where he became the American Air Force exchange officer on an Italian base. He spoke Italian 24/7. It was eight long months before we reconnected again, in Italy. We toured that beautiful country by car, and I became hooked on Italy. When my twin and I had traveled the Continent while college students, we had toured Italy, among other countries. We had disliked it because, at that time, for us, as single tall blonde twins, touring was unpleasant and challenging. We had had it. This time I saw Italy through different lenses, and I had a gentleman who spoke fluent Italian as my guide.

The Monterey TV station closed its doors due to poor management. It was a sad day for all. So, I returned to Sacramento and moved downtown. One Saturday I walked to the convention center where a health fair was being held. The booth that drew the most attention was a Nikken booth. [Nikken is a Japanese company that promotes wellness products such as pure healthy water, magnetic products, bio-ceramic technology products, and nutritionals.] The woman at the booth strongly suggested that I borrow the mattress pad for two weeks, so I could experience the benefits of the product. Being polite and not understanding what the products or company was all about, I accepted. To my amazement, I had an incredible product experience. In addition, I slept really well during that two-week period. Financially, and in my head, I was not ready to do anything with the products or company, and I definitely was not ready to make such a dramatic shift in wellness thinking and lifestyle. I did, however, attend one of their meetings and, hesitantly and cautiously bought a magnet designed for the lower back. After the scoliosis surgery, my lower back had discomfort more often than not, but using that magnet had seemed to ease the discomfort. Perhaps there was something to these magnetic products after all.

For two years, Tony and I dated long distance. Somehow we managed to meet up every four to six months, either in Italy or in California. I certainly learned about patience. And, yes, I frequently repeated my mantra: "This too shall pass." Initially, the months between visits seemed like forever, but time did pass. When Tony returned to the States at the end of his overseas tour, he got stationed in Florida. One month later, he surprised me by proposing. In hindsight, I realized that all those "lost" job interviews in Sacramento were because God had other plans for me: I was meant to meet Tony in Monterey. When I finally realized this, I had understanding and *gratitude*.

Tony and I planned our wedding so we would get married on Armed Forces Day of the next year. In addition to planning the wedding long distance, I decided to get my Masters in Education. I thought, as a military spouse, with this advanced degree, I would be more marketable. I worked as a substitute teacher during the day, attended night school in the evenings, and worked at a TV production studio a couple of Saturdays a month. The night school schedule was very accelerated – a new class and subject matter every month. In my first class, I met Mary, a fellow student and a mentor teacher at her school. She helped me return to the mindset of being a student. She also informed me after our fourth class together that, if I continued to earn an "A" in all my classes, I would graduate with honors. And so I did. As did she. I have utilized the knowledge gleaned from my education many a time, but decided not to return to the field of education as my interests ultimately moved in other directions.

Tony and I had a military wedding in Ann Arbor, with family and friends coming from literally all over the states and the world. Among those who flew in were Gloria, my German girlfriend; Sharon, my dear friend from California; one of Tony's sisters from Cape Verde, where she was working in the Peace Corps; and Barbara's fiancé, from Korea, where he was stationed. Tony and I honeymooned in Italy, first spending time on the Amalfi Coast and then visiting Italian buddies Tony had made while he was an exchange officer. The point to this story is we made a detour trip to Naples to get military gas coupons, which were available only to active duty folks. The day was overcast, and at times we got discombobulated on the narrow, cobblestone streets. I drove the rental car because I love driving a stick shift on winding roads. We eventually arrived on the base, got gas, and walked around. Suffice it to say, I was not impressed with Naples or the military base, and as we were driving out of Naples, I adamantly exclaimed to my new husband that I NEVER, ever wanted to get stationed there. He felt confident we wouldn't because it was a Navy base. We are Air Force. Whew, I dodged that bullet.

A couple of years after the Sacramento health fair experience, I was married and living in Florida. One weekend, my new husband and I traveled to Mobile, Alabama, to participate in a running/walking race. He ran the 5K race. I race-walked and won in my age category. Yeah! Coordinated with this event was an outdoor health festival.

Who had a booth there? None other than a Nikken representative. We chatted for a while, and she was impressed that I knew so much about the products. Nevertheless, I had no desire to work with her or under her in the business. The next month, I participated in yet another walking race where another Nikken representative was actually loaning out products. I borrowed one of their knee wraps and again had an impressive product experience. Within the week I, too, became a Nikken representative. I quickly became totally, and I do mean totally, engrossed with the Nikken wellness products. According to some friends and relatives, I ate and slept Nikken ad nauseam. Bless them for their patience and understanding – and for still being my friend. *Gratitude.*

By embracing all that was Nikken, I learned two things: a new lifestyle of sorts (it increased my awareness regarding health and wellness) and, definitely, a new way of thinking...a spiritual and metaphysical way of thinking. It was tough to shift how I looked at life. I had thought my lifestyle was healthy; I had thought my way of thinking was positive. Gosh, did I have a lot to learn.

For one of my in-home presentations, I invited so many people I thought it would be standing room only. Even though most of them said they "might" or "will try" to attend, to my immense disappointment, only a handful of folks showed up. One of my mentors, Naomi, had to repeatedly inform and reassure me that all was truly well. Those who came were meant to come. Huh? (Keep in mind this was a totally new way of thinking for me.) This is what I learned: The words "try" and "might" do not have a place in the world of doers. The subconscious mind does not process those words. The word "try" is the equivalent of saying "no." If I can quote Yoda from "The Empire Strikes Back": "Do...or do not. There is no try." I also learned it is always incumbent on me to present a wonderful, energized presentation to whomever attends an event, for those are the ones who want to hear what you have to say. One ought not waste time bemoaning those who did not attend.

A month and a half after we got married, my active duty husband was away for a few weeks. On my way to my Red Cross volunteer job on base, I was involved in a serious, near head-on collision. My beautiful Saab, according to the insurance adjuster, saved me from serious injury, maybe even death. My car spun. The small truck that hit me flipped. I was taken to a base hospital, not the base I was going to, but one further away, one with an emergency room. I sustained minor injuries, yet the military folks would send me home only after they had located my husband via telephone, and that took what seemed like an eternity. Since I was so new to the area, I knew few people who could take me home. The person who finally did take me home was a Colonel who knew my husband. The poignant part of this story is that his wife was dying of cancer. Nevertheless, he got me home and made sure I was okay. Then, for the next two weeks, a volunteer co-worker, whose family life was sad and complicated, called on me every day, even getting me out of the house. A blessing. *Gratitude.*

I called Sharon, my dear friend in California, and told her the news about my accident. What I remember most from that conversation was her statement that the accident was a blessing. What???!! My beloved car was smooshed, and she was telling me it was a...blessing? Yet, her words snapped me into attention. She said that, although what happened was terrifying and awful, I had no broken bones and no one had died. My Saab had been stalling and causing me lots of money in repairs. What if I had been driving at night, alone on the dark highway, when it stalled? I did not have a cell phone at the time. Talking to Sharon was another blessing. I have such *gratitude* that she is in my life.

During this time, I was introduced consciously to the concept of a gratitude list. Introduced is a pleasant word. Smacked on the head is more like it. The day after the accident, the man we had hired to put in a lawn irrigation system came by to start work on the project. He did not recognize me. Apparently, I looked pretty shattered, and his crew thought they were seeing a ghost. Why? Because they had been within half a block of the accident when it happened. They had heard the crash. They had seen the vehicles. They had seen the driver being removed from the Saab on a stretcher, not moving. Although they did not know it was me at the time, I was, apparently, their topic of conversation the remainder of that day. By the look of the car, they thought the driver (me) was dead.

The man we had hired (I will refer to him as "Mr. Kind Boss Man") ended up driving me to the car wreck place to clear out my belongings from the Saab. I cried the entire time, and because it was raining, I felt the heavens were feeling my emotional and physical pain. Mr. Kind Boss Man stated that my gratitude list was long. I did not understand what he was talking about, so he had to explain it. All I could think about was my smooshed beloved Saab, the deep (and I mean *deep*) bruises, the aches, and the swollen areas, not to mention the fact my husband was still out of state. Mr. Kind Boss Man informed me that my injuries, in the big picture of life, were minor, that the other driver walked away with no apparent injuries, that no one else was involved, that only our vehicles were affected, and that no lives were lost. Wow. I had not thought of it that way, thinking only of the positive. Thank you. A blessing. *Gratitude.*

As I was recuperating from the accident, I had a monumental "ah-ha" moment. *Monumental.* My mind flashed back to the moment I almost bumped into the future Lady Diana in London. When she died in that horrific car crash in Paris, I was traumatized like the rest of the world. I was also stunned that a Mercedes could crumble so incredibly. From that time on, I wondered, "What is it like to be in a bad accident?" And I allowed that thought to play around in the back of my mind over the years. Well, I surely did experience what it was like! As part of my "awakening" to the spiritual and metaphysical way of thinking, it occurred to me that, energetically, I had attracted this accident to me! I was speechless and mortified at the thought. Oh, my. What an eye-opener. What we dwell on, we attract.

Back to Sacramento briefly.... I got married four months before my twin, and, on a sidenote, we both married military men. I flew to Sacramento to assist her in her wedding preparations. Because I had some free time, I visited with Penny, my friend from the church choir in Sacramento. She was a soloist in the choir, a veteran, a military "brat" (her Dad was military), an educator, and a remarkable woman. Among the many topics of conversation we covered were her knee issues. I mentioned, of course, all the wonderful Nikken products for healing. To my surprise, Penny, who is open-minded and forthright, responded that she had, to no avail, tried everything to ease the discomfort of her knees – even the Nikken products. What she proceeded to share with me stuck with me. She said that despite all the medications she had taken, all the holistic products she had tried, and all the everything she had tried, had not worked, she had realized, with her own big "ah-ha" moment, that the discomfort must be generating from her subconscious mind! At this time in her life, there were several challenges – both personal and job related – she needed to overcome. Penny understood the correlation of the mind and body before I had even made a conscious connection between the two.

Within a few months of getting married, we discovered that I was pregnant. When I say "discovered," it is in the true sense of the word. We found out the day before Thanksgiving when I went to the doctor to figure out why I was feeling so sluggish and bloated. The doctor informed me that I was at the end of my first trimester, beginning the fourth. Wow. What a Thanksgiving gift. The following day, Tony left for Europe for four months of military work. Within weeks, I miscarried. The fetus had no heartbeat. The doctor and I chose to do a medical procedure rather than allow nature to take its course because I was about to head off to Europe, traveling mostly solo on trains for the next month. To naturally miscarry would not be in my best interest. That may sound selfish, but I know that, for me, I made the right decision.

As I was being wheeled away into surgery, I wailed to my parents that I was so sorry. They just happened to be visiting (*gratitude*), which was good since my husband was out of the country. The baby was to have been my parents' only natural born grandbaby. (My brother had adopted two little ones from Russia.) I was completely, absolutely inconsolable. Within ten days after the procedure, I was in Europe visiting my husband and friends. In time, I believed I had dealt with the emotions of the miscarriage.

When I returned from visiting my new husband in Europe, I had a doctor's appointment for a regular checkup. The civilian doctor was retired military and her nurse assistant was a military spouse. The nurse asked me how I was doing, and without skipping a beat, I replied, "Great!" She pointed out what my last year had been like: I had been in a serious auto accident; two months later, I had to evacuate with friends, including our visiting Italian teenage guest, to escape my very first hurricane; I had experienced a fierce storm with hail (unheard of in Florida); and I had suffered a miscarriage – all within eight months of marriage and all without my husband. I was alone in Florida, with no family members from either side within a two-day drive (except my parents were with me for the miscarriage). With immense kindness, this lovely nurse instructed me to allow myself to cry. She told me not to be a stoic military wife, but to cry, cry, cry. In hindsight, this nurse was a blessing. *Gratitude.* I now see how much of the stuffed emotions could have created, or were in the process of creating symptoms or dis-ease.

About this time, I was meeting many folks who were sharing with me how they had found God. They suggested I should also find God, and be born again, as they had been, in order to have a fulfilling life of peace. I searched for God in my mind. I struggled with this. What was I missing?! My first time at a particular health food store, I met a woman who occasionally worked there doing a type of health scanning. We bonded immediately and found we enjoyed each other's company. During one of my visits, I shared my find-God journey with her. With a knowing, loving chuckle, she gently informed me that I had never "lost" God. I did not have to "find" God, as I had never "left" Him! Ahhhh. An enormous wave of peace flowed over me as another "ah-ha" moment occurred. I had been following everyone else's path in search of my own. Just because someone else, whom I might respect, shared their personal journey and told me I *needed* to do the same, did not mean that I, Susan, was on that same path! *Gratitude.*

We had been married two years when Tony came home early with a huge grin on his face, barely able to contain his excitement. He asked me how I would like to live in Italy. I grilled him, wanting to know what city we would be stationed at. To every base I could think of, he responded with a shake of the head. Finally, it occurred to me that the only place I had not mentioned was Naples. Why would we ever go there? It was Navy and we were Air Force! What I did not know at the time was that Naples also had a North Atlantic Treaty Organization (NATO) base. Tony had been asked if he wanted to be assigned as an Air Force representative in NATO. He said I had two weeks to decide. When I told my mother this, she sent me a copy of Frances Mayes' book, *Under the Tuscan Sun*. Although we were not going to live in Tuscany, reading that book helped me make my decision. Before the end of the two weeks, I agreed to go to Naples.

[Personal note here.... After we had been married for at least 10 years, it came out in a conversation with friends that Tony had already agreed to go to Naples before he asked me about it. He wanted me to believe I had some "buffer" time to think it through, but he knew in his heart I would agree. Yup, I sure did. Some of our fondest memories are from living in Italy.]

Tony and I celebrated our third wedding anniversary shortly after arriving in Naples, Italy. Our tour of duty of just over three years was one huge gratitude, quite honestly, with lots of faith. That does not mean there were not some challenging moments.

For a solid month we looked with military-sponsored Italian realtors at over 50 places to live. No place seemed right. People told us we would have to compromise. And I flatly refused. Why should I compromise? I believed that the "right" place had yet to be found. One day during our search, we passed an attractive, elegant, gated *parco* (subdivision). To my disappointment, the realtor stated that there was nothing available there. In time, Tony found a place while I was at an appointment. Due to a scheduling conflict, he could only take me to see the apartment at night. As a result, I was unable to see the view that made Tony so excited about the place. It had parquet floors, curved wooden doors and doorways, and large rooms. And, in every room, very tall double doors opened onto a wide balcony. Because of Tony's excitement, beyond the immediate architecture and design, I had to trust his opinion. We agreed to take the place. The landlady seemed to be pleasant enough. Once I went there during the daytime, and could find my bearings, I realized this was the same *parco* I had pointed out earlier! *Intention and faith.*

Oh, how I loved that apartment! It was the top floor of a villa where our landlady lived. The villa used to be her family home. When her husband died she had renovated the villa so she could rent out the upstairs. Our floor used to be her children's rooms and the family room. Our view was of the Bay of Naples, Vesuvius, and Capri. The flat roof was also "ours" and offered a 360-degree view of the area, and what a view it was. Spectacular doesn't even come close to expressing what we saw every day. *Gratitude.*

Tony loved that the landlady, Stamira, and I got along so well – despite the fact my Italian was negligible at the time and she knew only a handful of English words: "please, open, thank you, okay." Using the little bit of high school French I remembered, Stamira and I would chat. She would speak in Italian and French, and I would speak in French and English. Somehow we communicated. *Gratitude.* In time, I learned enough Italian to carry on a basic conversation.

One evening, approximately a month after moving in, Tony and I were going out to dinner and ran into Stamira on the stairway. We invited her to join us for dinner so we could celebrate a big moment. Before we had even explained what we were celebrating, she said to Tony (he being fluent in Italian) that she could see in my eyes I had gotten a car. Yes, she was correct, but how did she know that? We had bought a used car for me, and I was excited. It was an Alfa Romeo and a stick shift, as most cars were at the time. *Ahhh, la mia bella macchina.* (My beautiful car.)

Every day in Italy was an adventure. I took each day as it came, and all the adventures as they presented themselves. I could write a huge book of memoirs, but this book is not the place to include it all. Just the highlights.

Late one Friday afternoon, Tony and I drove to the Amalfi coast, to the town of Ravello where there was to be an early evening outdoor classical concert. It was a big deal. We arrived early so we drove around, exploring. We drove up and down little roads, checking out the houses and the views. One road turned out to be an incredibly steep private driveway for a couple of houses. As I turned the car around to go back up that incredibly steep driveway, the clutch did not want to cooperate. As a woman who prides herself on her driving abilities, I was "sweating bullets." I reluctantly asked my husband to take over. By the grace of God, he got that car up the incredibly steep drive. I happily walked up, full of *gratitude.*

Then, while we were still meandering, the car got a flat tire! There we were, all dressed up for an elegant concert, with Tony looking so handsome in his suit. Without hesitating, he changed that tire with ease and grace and did not get a touch of dirt or grease on his clothing. My hero! *Gratitude.* It was as if the angels had protected his clothing and made changing the tire a simple event. Tony and I are still in awe of that flat tire event.

My father passed away while we were in Italy. The night before he died, Mom called to tell me it was time to come home because Dad was fading fast. The call I had been dreading came very early the next morning. I was so upset that he could not wait for us to return home. Then it dawned on me. He had not even waited for Mom and Barbara to return to the hospital, which was only a 15-minute drive away. Still, I was upset with him! As I think back, this absurd reaction was just a manifestation of my grief.

The next day we flew out of the Rome airport to return home for my Dad's funeral. Other than Tony and me, the only other person on the military chartered bus to the Rome airport was a nurse. In hindsight, this was providence. She suggested I read the book *Final Gifts: Understanding the Special Awareness, Needs, and Communications of the Dying*, written by two hospice workers, Maggie Callanan and Patricia Kelley. The nurse said the book had helped her, and it might help me accept the timing of my Dad's death.

My brother picked us up at the airport and took us immediately to the funeral home. The directors of the funeral home had waited for us to view my father's body before they cremated him. We were escorted to the basement of the funeral home. My brother held my one arm and my husband held the other. As I remember the experience, once downstairs, we entered a long, dark room. Dad was on a gurney at the far end, covered by a sheet with his shoulders and head visible. There was a spotlight on him. In the movie "The Wizard of Oz," there is a scene where Dorothy, the Scarecrow, and the Lion are walking toward the Wizard for the first time. The Lion turns around and runs out through a window. Well, that was sort of like me. I got free of my supporters, turned around, and walked rapidly in the other direction, saying, "That is not my Dad!" It was not him. It was only his body. He was no longer of this earth. My husband and brother had to come get me and once again escort me to the body of my Dad. Even so, I stayed for only a brief moment. I took a peek under the sheet to see how the funeral guys had placed Dad's arms and hands. They were gently folded over his chest. I don't know why that was important to me, but it was.

After we buried my father's ashes and returned to Italy, I ordered *Final Gifts*. I spent all my free time reading that book. It was emotional to say the least, but, truly, that book helped me heal from Dad's death. For one thing, it helped me realize that Dad had chosen to have none of us with him when he passed. It put so much into perspective for me. *Gratitude*. It also helped me, a little bit, to heal from the miscarriage. I felt so strongly about the "healingness" of this book that I ordered a box and handed the book out to relatives and friends in need. One of Tony's cousins read it and said she is forever grateful that I gave her the book when her Mom was ill and in the dying process. She, in turn, passed her book on to friends in need. The book ultimately prepared me to deal emotionally with the illness and passing of my Mom many years later. *Gratitude*.

Another bit of *gratitude,* in regards to the passing of my Dad, was that less than 10 minutes after we got the call about my Dad, a fellow military spouse and dear friend called. She needed to give me some information before I began my day. It was good information for me, but what made it so special, was that she was the first friend I was planning to call to share the news about my Dad. I just "knew" she was the one I wanted to call first. Yet, she had called me. The news she gave me was definitely not the kind of news that was 6 a.m. pertinent. Therefore, I believe, God had a hand in her calling me so early. The call was more than a coincidence.

When our time in Italy came to a close, I was beside myself with grief. There were so many people, so many things, I did not want to leave: Stamira, Italy in general, my NATO friends, and the European lifestyle that makes so much sense to me. The day the movers arrived, I began snapping at them, as well as Stamira. Yes, I admit it was bad. Tony had to pull me aside and ask what was going on. What I realized, but didn't want to acknowledge, was the message that it was time to go. During the last week in our villa apartment, a few items had begun to malfunction – one of the toilets, a tub drain, a window latch. The Universe was kind of kicking us out of Italy and on to new adventures. I understood it, even though I was not happy about it.

Once back in the States, I was numb, merely going through the motions of living. We were assigned to base housing our first night back. All the pent up emotions about leaving Italy were let loose like a burst water pipe when I saw a big cockroach in the bathtub. At least we could soon return to our former house that we had rented out. Within a week of our return, we had bought two new cell phones, a car for me, and an empty lot in a new subdivision. I soon got totally engrossed in working with and supplying the builder with various items for the house. I was finally back in my creative element. I spent as little time on base as I could and forged a new life outside the military family. I was still very much interested in the Japanese wellness products, but my myopic interest was waning. We have and use the products every day, yet, at that time, I was ready for something new.

One of my Nikken mentors lived in a nearby town. Every time she sent an e-mail message, she closed it with "Infinite Love & Gratitude." The first time I read that, I leaned back in my computer chair and said aloud, "Oh, my, Margie has really lost it!" Because she kept on using the phrase whenever she spoke or wrote an e-mail, I finally asked her about it. Before long, I was one of seven students who crammed into a friend's home in Chicago so we could all attend the first of three 3-day classes on a newish healing modality. Somehow it all worked out smoothly. We were literally camped out all over the house, a house that was already home to a husband and wife and their two adolescent kids. Ruth, the hostess, and Margie, had already completed the course and were certified practitioners. They were attending the class as assistants.

The class was taught by Dr. Darren R. Weissman, a chiropractor and holistic healer out of Chicago. I made sure I sat in a front row and was all ears. I was enthralled by this modality, the LifeLine Technique®, yet, for me at the time, it was a bit overwhelming. Nevertheless, I practiced on myself what I had learned so as to become more familiar with it.

About a year later, Margie introduced me to another healing modality, The Emotion Code, created by Dr. Bradley Nelson, also a chiropractor and holistic healer. At the request of a friend, Dr. Nelson flew to Chicago, in the bitter cold of January, for a one-time class event. It was a small – and, I'd go so far as to say, intimate – class, with no more than 20 people attending. Of course, I sat in one of the first few rows. It's like church or theatre. If I'm going to attend an event, I want to be in the first few rows. That way I am a participant, not just an observer. What a fantastic class it was. By the time I flew home, I felt like I could teach the class. I was hooked.

I quickly became not only certified, but also proficient at the Emotion Code. I worked with anyone who would allow me. I was very confident in muscle testing, too. My beloved husband was proud of me, so proud that, against my wishes, he signed me up to have a booth at the next local metaphysical fair just a mile from our house. He believed I was good enough to start doing emotional release healing as a business. It was a two-day event. On the morning the event started, Tony and I argued in the car on the way there, and we argued as we were setting up our table. Luckily, a friend of ours, who had initially suggested I work at this fair, had her table next to ours. She did energy healing where she moved her hands around a person. The fair began and no one visited our table. They passed us by, not even looking in our direction! By this time I was not only aggravated, I was also bummed. This confirmed that I was not ready to do this, or so I thought. I asked our friend if she could do whatever she does and remove any negative energy from me. A minute later, I was back at my table. Then, I asked if she would work with Tony, who had remained with me as my support system. I was so thankful for her help. I kid you not, as she was working on Tony, I had my first client – and I was busy the rest of the event. *Gratitude.*

Fast forward a few years…. I decided to pursue the long training process to become a Certified LifeLine Practitioner (CLP). As part of our training, it was highly recommended that we experience this modality of healing with other CLPs. Well, not once, but during three of the sessions I participated in, various emotions dealing with the miscarriage came up. Each time, I wailed and wailed and wailed. I seemed to have a bottomless pit of tears. Apparently, I had attempted to be the stoic military spouse for my new husband as I suffered privately. So much for believing I had dealt with all the emotions concerning the miscarriage.

I am sharing this personal story because I want you, the reader, to know that, even if you truly believe that you have dealt with a situation emotionally, there is a very good chance that, within your core, you have not. I honestly believed that I had completely dealt with the deep sorrow of my miscarriage and other related emotions. What an eye-opener I had when, not once, but three times with three different practitioners, I released so many deeply trapped emotions. I know I have now healed from the miscarriage. It was an unfortunate event in my life, but I can now talk about it without getting teary-eyed or feeling a deep, deep sadness.

The training for the LifeLine Technique®, in my opinion, was intense. Rather than get totally intimidated, I went at it gung ho. I worked with a few study buddies, had several sessions with other CLPs, and joined an eleventh-hour study group. By the time the written exam, called the Celebration of Learning, took place, I was ready. It was an incredibly long written exam. When I finished, I went to the ladies room. A few women had gathered to complain about the exam and how awful it was. Excuse me? If they had actually studied, they would have known the material. Besides, we were told what to study, so it was only a matter of doing it. As soon as I heard what they were saying, I rushed out of the restroom as fast as I could. I did not want to hear any more negativity. It would be contagious if I allowed it to be, and I, at the moment, was bursting with a feeling of accomplishment. By the way, I received a 99% score on that handwritten exam.

Positive thinking is so important. When I get into a low energy/low vibration, unhappy, irritated mood, I allow myself to briefly, no more than 24 hours, wallow in the emotional gunk. Then, I make sure I move forward and out of it. If I let myself start dwelling on the negativity, I would or could get into a tailspin. Therefore, I do my best to get into positive thinking and do so in a number of ways. I may do emotional release healing on myself, or I literally make myself find the goodness in little things. For instance, when I am out driving, if the stop light is green, that is a positive. If I am looking for a parking spot near a shop entrance and find one, that is a positive thing. And so it goes. Maintain *gratitude*.

A story on positive thinking and parking.... When I am out and about in search of a "good" parking spot, I ask my Dad, who passed years ago, for a parking spot. He always had a knack for finding a good one in a timely manner. In addition, I ask God and my guardian angels to find a good parking spot for me. Of course, I also create a little mantra on getting a good spot. Without fail, a good spot soon appears. *Gratitude, and, faith.*

Only one time did that specific request "fail" me. My husband and I were on a road trip to California. One of the cities we visited was Sacramento, where I used to live. We had planned to go to dinner in the Old Sacramento area of town, but the place was full of dressed up teenagers. The activity level was so high, we knew it was not a typical night. We finally learned it was prom night. We could not find a parking spot – anywhere. I could not even create a spot with a teeny bit of space. My parking mantra wasn't working. Without dwelling on our supposed misfortune, we drove to a different area of town a few blocks away. Apparently, God had other plans for us. We immediately found a parking spot almost in front of one of our favorite restaurants! As we were waiting to be seated, we chatted with the maître d' for a few minutes. To our delight, that month the restaurant was promoting cuisine from the region in Italy where my husband's family is from. Plus, the head chef of the entire restaurant organization turned out to be a man from the village of Tony's family, a guy my husband knew. We were meant to be at that restaurant that night. *Gratitude.*

One evening, when I was still new to practicing Reiki, I decided to practice on my husband. My hands came to the area around his heart. Almost immediately, I began to get teary eyed. Not knowing what to do with this, I pulled away and soon ended the session. I said nothing. About a week later, the same thing happened. This time I mentioned it to my husband, and that was that. What did we know? I was soon to find out.

We started a healing circle in our home. It began with a handful of healers from various modalities who worked with each other in turn. Eventually, the group grew so large it was evident we needed to change venues. A fellow healer had just moved into a large rental house. I assisted her in painting the room that she planned to use for healing. Our healing group then moved into this much larger room. *Gratitude.*

One night, Tony and I walked into the house where the healing circle was taking place, and I felt a bit uneasy. I felt uncomfortable (it was the negative energy) as I walked through the kitchen where the hostess was chatting with a married couple new to the group. The husband was one of the first to get on a massage table for healing. He was a total nonbeliever and had a lot of doubt and even anger. I did emotional release healing on him and let others practice their specific energy healing modality. After several emotions were released, I began to weep. The weeping turned into sobs, and the sobs turned into wailing as I dashed out of the room, gasping for breath. At each stage of my emotions, the man was also expressing himself by deep, heavy sighs. Simultaneously, to my running out of the room, the guy sat up and also began wailing. Then he fell back onto the message table. When I ran out of the room, I was almost frantic, not knowing what to do with the tremendous surge of grief. All I could think of to do was to wash my hands in ice cold water, and that calmed me down almost immediately. When I returned, this guy reached out his hand to me and said, "Thank you." *Hhmmm.* Apparently what I had done was to energetically assist him in releasing some past life trauma. About a year later, the man became a healer himself. *Gratitude.*

Around the time of that healing, I began experiencing that odd teary-eyed feeling more and more often when I worked with someone. With the guidance of some of the healers in our healing group, I learned that I am empathic. That means I am able to understand someone else's unspoken feelings or emotions. It also means I can be very sensitive, which can be a very good thing or a not so good thing. I thus do my best to not take things personally. And, I must remember to always put an energetic field around myself so I do not absorb others' energy (but sometimes I forget). Many times I have had to ask my higher self if a particular feeling, such as a sudden pain in the abdomen, is mine or coming from someone else. Most of the time, it is coming from someone else.

In time, I reluctantly came to the conclusion that it was necessary for me to have a hip replacement. For years, I stayed in denial – until I could barely walk. The surgery was scheduled for the spring of that year. I was to be the poster child for a quick recovery because of my activity level and the energy work I practice. The surgeon was the head of the department and was well respected. I knew folks who had had their hips replaced by him and they had recovered beautifully. Prior to surgery, I did a significant amount of healing work on myself, releasing trapped emotions present and past, even distant past lives.

When I was wheeled into the operating room, I was naturally a tad nervous, yet I was confidant all would be well.

Except that it was not. A long and painful four months later, the surgeon said something was not right, and we had to go back in. Why he did not notice that something was not right within two weeks post-op is beyond my comprehension. Prior to learning another surgery was required, and obviously before I learned what the medical error was, my dear LifeLine Technique® study buddy, Jan, who lives in Canada, worked with me doing emotional release work to help in the healing process. This is important for the reader to know, too, because these sessions were difficult for me to do. At one point, Jan instructed me to say "I love you, hip." Hesitantly, I whimpered in response, "*^%$#@*&!!! you". Bless her heart, Jan is so patient and loving. She worked with me for many sessions. Thankfully, we are friends to this day. *Gratitude.*

Although she and I cleared a lot of emotions and reactionary patterns, I must admit the hip could not be healed only by releasing emotions. There were major physical issues to be addressed with surgery. Then, the day of that second surgery, shortly after being wheeled into my room, the nurse came in and slightly adjusted my body. Before she even had a chance to leave the room, I heard a snap, pop and ripping sound and experienced the most excruciating pain. Lordy, was it painful, like giving birth to a hippo. I screamed and hollered for the nurse to call the surgeon. She looked at me and walked out the door. The next morning, when the surgeon was doing his rounds, I informed him of the night's event because, apparently, the nurse had not called him. He brushed me off saying that the new joint was not going anywhere and all would be well.

A day after surgery, I received a phone call informing me that my Mom had suffered a minor stroke that affected her speech. There was obviously nothing I could do but pray. That night, a nurse, thinking she was helping, offered to give me a sleeping pill. Hesitantly and feeling helpless I thought, *"Heck, why not add one more pill to the mix of post-op drugs?"* I hoped it would help me get some sleep. The next morning I awoke early. My head felt heavy from the drugs, my Mom still had the stroke, and I was still stuck in the hospital. No change in my life. The sleeping pill was but a placebo in the long run. Mom was stable and doing well, so Barbara flew down to take care of me once I got the okay to return home from two weeks in rehab. I was home perhaps a week when we got another call informing us that Mom had suffered a major stroke that severely damaged her brain. I was unable to travel for a week, but once I got permission to be a passenger in a car for the two-day car ride, Barbara and I drove to Ann Arbor to be with Mom.

Depending on one's point of view, the drive to Michigan was an adventure. At least that is how I chose to look at it. We had to stop at every rest area – located about one to two hours apart the entire length of the trip – so I could move the hip muscles that cramped up so readily. Maneuvering the walker was tricky, and, by then, I had forgotten about the pop and ripping sound from the first day of surgery. I was in constant pain.

Barbara and I arrived in Michigan and immediately drove to the hospital in a nearby town where Mom had been taken after her stroke. There I was with my walker, gingerly taking every painful step as I shuffled down the hospital corridor to see my Mom. I must have been a sight, dressed in street clothes but moving like I belonged in a hospital bed. Despite my pain and sorrow, I found myself chuckling at the visual image.

Earlier I mentioned finding the blessings, finding gratitude, even in awful events. When my Mom suffered the mild stroke that affected her speech, she lived in a condo for retired University of Michigan alumni. Sensing something was wrong, Mom went next door to her neighbors. The neighbor's grown children just happened to be visiting. Their two sons were clueless to Mom's symptoms. However, the daughter was a nurse and knew immediately what was going on. *Gratitude.* They called an ambulance, and off Mom went to the hospital. *Gratitude.* She worked hard with speech therapy and within a month was well on her way to full recovery. As she recovered and went through rehab, she was in the hospital rehab wing. The last time I talked with Mom, only complex concepts stumped her thinking. Otherwise, she talked and comprehended normally. *Gratitude* The week she was to be released, she suffered the stroke that damaged most of her brain. It had bothered me for months that I did not know who had found her, how long she had been alone after the stroke, etc. All of us kids lived out of state. It would be days before any of us could get to see her. What I learned, once we were with her, still brings tears of *gratitude* to my eyes.

A nurse happened to be passing Mom's room and glanced in just in time to see Mom walking and then falling flat forward like a board. Lickety split, that nurse was at Mom's side. A blessing. Mom was transported from rehab to the emergency room. Early in the morning, a family friend, who worked in the hospital as a physical therapist, stayed with Mom for almost eight hours, on her day off, despite the fact that she was having a dinner party that night. As she finished her unspoken "shift," one of my mother's dear friends took over for the next several hours – until Mom was transported to another hospital in a nearby town. A blessing. There were no beds available for Mom at the first hospital due to its being the staging hospital for a meningitis outbreak. This second friend stayed with Mom into the evening hours at the second hospital. A blessing. *Immense gratitude.*

Barbara and I visited Mom every day at the second hospital. Eventually, she was transported back to Ann Arbor to a long-term rehab facility that had just been built. There she had a loving staff who took great care of her. A blessing. Because I was in Ann Arbor for an extended time, I was able to arrange physical therapy for my hip in the out-patient section of Mom's rehab facility. *Gratitude.*

SUSAN OLENCKI GIANGIULIO

After a month or two, overseeing Mom's care with my Barbara, I flew to Florida and continued with my physical therapy. This was a pattern I repeated several times over the next nine months (traveling between the two states). Still, even after all this therapy, and sometimes painful therapy, the healing just wasn't taking place. The surgeon paid no heed to that. Finally, just before he retired, I saw him one last time. He was stumped as to why I was not healing well, almost eight months after the second surgery. He acknowledged that there was a bulge that ought not to be where it was. Thinking it was displaced fat, he sent me to a plastic surgeon. The plastic surgeon informed me that it was displaced muscle! Now it all made sense to me, all the pain and lack of healing. Eventually, I was sent to another surgeon who worked out of another hospital.

I liked the new surgeon immediately. He was a traumatic injury specialist with a humanitarian heart. In fact, he had volunteered time in Haiti after the 2010 earthquake. And, he actually listened to me. But before I could follow up on our plan of action, I needed to return to Ann Arbor.

Toward the end of Mom's life, she was placed in hospice care at the facility. With us visiting every day, the addition of hospice care, and the assigned facility staff, Mom had marvelous care. Barbara and I began to prepare for Mom's impending death. At the funeral home we chose, I was drawn to the perfect ash box for Mom. Because it was all but hidden in a dark corner, the only one not in the catalogue, the only one without a price tag, and one that the director had never seen before, I knew that Mom's guardian angel directed me to it.

In the end, three members of the staff were with us when Mom passed. A blessing. *Immense gratitude.* Months later, Barbara and I returned to thank Mom's staff for their great care of Mom, as well as of us. They appreciated our thoughtfulness because, apparently, once a patient dies, family members rarely return to thank any of the staff.

Were there some challenging moments with staff during Mom's stay at the long-term care facility? You bet. Did we dwell on them? No. We rectified the challenges as soon as we could. We did our best to find the goodness in all aspects of this sad experience.

After my Dad died, Mom had created a file with instructions we would need after her death, including her wish to be cremated. In that file was all the information about the cemetery in Chicago, the city where she and Dad were born. It also contained an autobiography, and songs and readings she wished to have for her funeral mass, and the names of those she wished to do readings. *Gratitude.* The funny part, well it really wasn't humorous-funny, was that almost all of the designated folks were no longer of this earth. Nevertheless, my twin and I, who were in charge of planning the memorial mass and celebration of life, somehow got a plan together with greater ease than anticipated.

At the memorial mass, Tony, Barbara, and I, accompanied by a soloist and a pianist, all sang an *a cappella* song. We sang from our hearts and it felt so good. (People wondered if it was hard to sing at my Mom's memorial mass. No, it was not. I've sung at the funeral mass of several friends and relatives. One does their best to be in-the-moment of the music, not the venue.) The mass, if I may say so, was perfect – joyful and uplifting. It felt like a wedding mass. In fact, folks came up to us and commented that it was what they wanted for their funeral or memorial mass. Following the mass was the celebration of life reception. Oh, my gosh. We succeeded in creating another remarkable event. Again, folks came up to us and commented on how uplifting the event was, and on the fact they felt the joy in the room. Yes, we were celebrating Mom's life. She would be so proud of us. And I knew in my heart that Barbara and I had done our best, and a remarkable job we did! As I write this, I feel goose bumps, tears of joy, and *gratitude.*

We buried my Mom's ashes in Chicago with the ashes of my Dad. Afterward, we kids wanted to see the last member of our parents' generation, Felicia, one of my mother's cousins. However, Felicia was in the hospital recovering from surgery. We were friendly with one of her daughters, Kathie, and, at that time, only knew Kathie's sister and brother by sight. Kathie encouraged us to visit her mom, but the other sister said it would be too much for her mom to have so many visitors at once. Kathie prevailed. We had a plan. We would all (my brother Tom and his family, Barbara, Tony and me, and Kathie) go to the hospital. Kathie would go up to her Mom's room and check to see if it was okay with the mother for us to visit. In the meantime, the rest of us would all be waiting in the lobby downstairs. Here's the amazing part. My Mom wanted us to be there. How did I, Kathie, and my twin "know" this? As we were walking in the parking lot to the hospital, we saw a car parked with a personal license plate of "Irene" – my Mom's name – so close to the entrance it was uncanny! The three of us girls did a unified high five. Felicia was pleased and touched to see all of us. Thanks, Mom. *Gratitude.*

Right after burying my Mom's ashes, I underwent the three tests my new surgeon wanted me to do so he could verify the possibilities of why there were still issues with the hip. Well, ten days after getting the results, I was once again in surgery! This wonderful, skilled surgeon repaired as best as possible, seriously damaged soft tissue that had been continuously aggravated – and not diagnosed – for over a year. Well, well. No wonder the soft tissue had not healed. There was no way it could ever have healed.

Once again, my twin came down to assist me in my recuperation. *Gratitude beyond infinite.* I spent two weeks in a rehab facility, anticipating my road to recovery, once and for all. I chose to go to the rehab facility to get over the hump from all the drugs, and to get a handle on physical therapy and occupational therapy because I was to be in an immobility brace for multiple weeks. I was told I would not like this brace as it went from my torso to below my knee. To the contrary. I grew to appreciate it. It was a means to an end; using it became second nature. *It is what it is. This too shall pass. Forward and onward.*

I still work at being able to walk with ease, jump, climb stairs, and walk short distances solo. It is constant work and sometimes not pleasant. I do emotional release healing every day. I have my down moments, but my husband and others who have been with me through this journey, lift me up during times of frustration. We celebrate the tiniest bits of healing. *Gratitude.* One surgeon's "mistake," or whatever one wishes to call it, has changed my life forever. So, I now look at what the lessons are for me and/or for those around me. It is yet another adventure. It is a new way of life and I deal with it the best I can, every day. At least I am able to walk, and to walk without immense discomfort.

A few years later, I met a healer whose forte was connecting to Quan Yin, the Goddess of Mercy and Compassion, a revered East Asian deity. I was curious about what they both had to say to me. The session was short and to the point. I left feeling euphoric and emotionally drained at the same time. I was told I was strongly connected to Mother Mary. Her arms are always supporting me and protecting me. When I heard this, I teared up. Teared up with understanding and joy. I connected to that statement so intensely. It made so much sense to me. *Gratitude.* As I was preparing to visit Tony for the first time while we were dating and he was living in Italy, I had decided to wear, as a protective and decorative talisman, a tiny necklace with a small turquoise cloisonné charm with Mother Mary on the front and Pope John XXIII on the other side. It was purchased in Rome, in the Vatican, during my first trip to Italy as a child. Up until that point, I had never paid it much heed. For some reason, I had a need to start wearing it on my trip to see Tony. That was the beginning of my connection to Mother Mary, yet I was not consciously aware of it. Wow, what one recognizes in hindsight. In time I realized that I need not always wear that necklace to be connected to her. If Mother Mary is in my heart, and, my intention is such, then so it is.

During one of Barbara's visits, we took a road trip to southern Florida to meet up with friends and relatives we had not seen in years. The day after we arrived at our so-called base camp for touring, we drove an hour and a half in the pouring rain to meet up with a dear cousin. She, in turn, also drove an hour and a half, so we could meet halfway from where she lived. Because Barbara and I were driving in unknown territory in the heavy rain, I asked God, my guardian angels, and Archangel Michael to put a protective bubble around my car. As we drove, for my peace of mind, I kept reaffirming silently, the actuality of a protective bubble. When we arrived at our destination, and we both took a huge sigh of relief, I mentioned to Barbara that I had asked for a protective bubble around our car. Her response? "I thought there was something different! There were no cars around us!" Very true indeed. A blessing! *Gratitude.*

A healer friend of mine became my mentor for several months before she moved away. One day she came over to play with my energetic fields as a way for me to experience energy movement. Unbeknownst to us, we forgot to get me totally grounded again. When we were done, I offered her a cappuccino. I can make a cappuccino with ease, as it is second nature for me to make a cappuccino or espresso. The problem that day was I started pinging from cabinet to cabinet, not knowing what I was doing. It was funny, yet it wasn't. I was not Susan. Then it dawned on both of us. I had not been completely grounded after we had played around with my energy fields. My friend grounded me, however she did it, and voila, I literally felt grounded and like myself again. I then prepared and served our café with all my ceremonial fanfare.

Both my parents experienced one form of arthritis or another. At one time, I believed that I, too, was prone to it. However, I am now of the belief that, due to my training and my "awakening" to a new way of thinking, I have the ability to shift this proneness to arthritis. The shift involves not just emotional release healing, but also my web of belief – or the totality of my belief systems – and how I perceive my environment. Hence, I have learned that, while the environment affects our genes, it is our perception of our environment which controls them.[38] Recognizing this powerful concept was a huge "ah-ha" moment for me, one that has truly shifted my perception of life in general. So, on rare occasions, whenever one of my fingers starts to exhibit arthritic symptoms (such as stiffness or discomfort), I immediately begin to do emotional release work on myself, and, before long, the symptoms are gone.

One time, close to Christmas, I wanted to decorate our house *à la* Martha Stewart. I had seen something in her magazine that she had created using spray paint and magnolia leaves, which are plentiful where we live. However, I was stumped and basically paralyzed psychologically to be creative. Silly girl. I had the tools and strategies to take care of this. So, of course, I worked on myself. Only one emotion came up: creative insecurity. Uhhh…yup. I kid you not, like a dark veil being removed from my brain, I immediately went out and about doing what I needed to do to create what Martha Stewart had created, as if I had been doing it all along. No issue of insecurity here. Voila! The resulting decoration was exquisite. *Gratitude.*

When I lived in Manhattan, I began to comprehend that everyone who has come into my life has come for a reason. This insight brings to mind Steve, a beloved neighbor in Manhattan who became a close friend. Around the time we met, he married a woman from Ann Arbor. Due to the fact that both his wife's father and my father worked at the University of Michigan, we knew some folks in common. Because he was older than Barbara and me, and had sons approximately our age, we began to call him Uncle Steve. Barbara and I were the daughters he never had. He and I tended to run into each other in the street. For a while, I seemed to only see him before, sometimes during, and always after a relationship ended. One time, Uncle Steve informed me that I was getting better at recovering from breakups. He was right. I noticed it, too. With each guy I dated, I began to rebound quicker and quicker. It was then that I realized that each guy who came into my life was there for me to learn from, perhaps (or not) more than for him to learn from me. Each experience was a stepping stone toward the person I was to ultimately marry. Even people, in general, were stepping stones of experience so that I could grow and learn as a person. It may sound crass and unfeeling, but think about it, especially from an energetic point of view. Wow, it made life so much easier – if and when I remembered the concept. *Gratitude.*

The following quote holds a succinct truth: How I live and celebrate my life is a choice.

> *Each time I've been confronted with difficult times, I find it easier to look for the positive within ... So much in life comes down to how we choose to act and react in every situation. We can let problems defeat us; or we can learn and grow, find hope and happiness, as we light the fire within and begin to live with passion.*
>
> *Let's celebrate life - each high of great success, each low of crushing loss - and gain wisdom and acknowledge with every moment as we strive.*
>
> ~ **D. Gary Young,** *The Essential Edge,* **March 2017**

11. Self-Muscle Testing

As soon as you trust yourself, you will know how to live.

~ Goethe

Muscle testing procedures are accepted techniques to find and fix body imbalances and spinal misalignments. However, Dr. Bradley Nelson, developer of *The Emotion Code*, explains it is not widely recognized or accepted that muscle testing be used to get information directly from the subconscious mind.

The muscle testing I am about to share with you is meant only for practical, everyday uses; it is not meant to diagnose dis-ease. I use muscle testing to find trapped emotions, to figure out if my body can metabolize a particular food, and to determine if something is good for my body.

There are several methods of muscle testing. If you are interested in learning the medical aspects of muscle testing, I recommend you do your own research.

The following are a few techniques and tips for self-muscle testing:

1. Attempt to do all the techniques. Everyone develops their favorites.

2. As you ask yourself questions during the process, remember "yes" and "true" are used interchangeably, as are "no" and "false."

3. When practicing, if you find it challenging to differentiate the responses, practice teaching your body what a "yes" and

a "no" response ought to look like with each technique. To teach your body what a "yes" response is, actively create what a "yes" response feels and looks like by asking questions that have an **obvious** "yes" answer. In other words, ask questions or make statements that you know are true. Do the same for a "no" response by asking or making statements that you know are false.

4. Practice, practice, practice. Sometimes it may take you several weeks to get the hang of one technique, so, please, be patient. Do not fret over the time it takes. And please, there is no need to be hard on yourself. One day it will just click, and you will wonder what the big deal was. If one technique does not "click with you, or you really cannot get the hang of it, move on to another one. Soon you will find the one that best suits you. *Yeah!*

5. It is also a good idea to actually say the words "ego free" when self-muscle testing. Remember that muscle testing is not about your conscious-mind preferences, desires, or expectations. It is about what is in the best interest of your body. Your higher self knows what is best for you.

6. Always make sure you are hydrated with good, pure water (not distilled, which has no nourishing properties).

7. Take your time when muscle testing. Allow a second or two between the question and the actual testing. This gives your mind and body time to connect.

Which technique do I use? I use several. Initially, I learned the "bent arm" technique and then the "interlocking circle" technique because those who taught me used them almost exclusively. However, over time, I discovered the "finger flick" and the "finger slide," which can be done inconspicuously in public and using one hand. The "sway test" is the most basic technique, and the one that many people feel the most comfortable doing. Yes, I do that one, too.

Once you are hydrated, find a quiet space, and take a couple of deep breaths and relax. In other words, quiet your mind. When first learning how to self-muscle test, turn off the TV, radio, and other noises so that you can seriously concentrate. Once you learn and feel comfortable with at least one method, you will be able to do it quickly and with ease. Outside distractions will no longer matter as much. Yet, always quiet your mind. That is very important in order to connect with your higher self.

PLEASE NOTE: To reiterate, as stated in Step #5, it is a good idea to actually say the words "ego free" when self-muscle testing, at least until you become proficient at muscle testing. Remember, muscle testing is not about your conscious-mind preferences, desires, or expectations. It is about what is in the best interest of your body. Your higher self knows what is best for you.

To learn about the various emotions and how to release them, I suggest you study one or both healing modalities, The Emotion Code or the LifeLine Technique®. After all, this book is about energy and emotional release healing; however, this chapter is merely an introduction to self-muscle testing.

Okay, let's get started....

BASIC SWAY TEST

Stand to do the sway test.

1. Relax your whole body, feet about a hip width apart for balance.
2. Say "My name is _____."
3. Your body will sway forward as a "yes" response.
4. Say a false name with "My name is _____." You can even use an inanimate object as your false name.
5. Your body will sway backwards as a "no" response.

If there is no movement on "yes" and "no," teach your body what a "yes" and "no" response is.

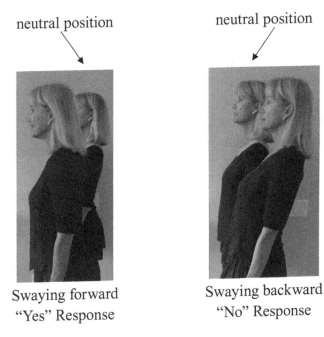

neutral position	neutral position
Swaying forward "Yes" Response	Swaying backward "No" Response

The person in the front represents you, the tester.

The person in the back, standing still, represents the baseline – the neutral position where you were.

TWO-HANDED TECHNIQUES

Bent Arm

1. Bend one arm at the elbow so the arm is at a 90-degree angle.

2. Place other hand just past the wrist bone, toward elbow side. I suggest using only two fingers for a lighter touch and less strain.

3. Say "My name is _____." Gently press hand on bent elbow arm.

4. The arm will stay strong and will not go weak, even if there is a slight give, with a "true" answer.

5. Give a totally false name. Gently press hand on bent elbow arm.

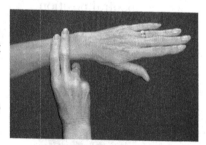

6. The arm will noticeably go weak with a "false" answer.

Interlocking Circles

1. Make a circle with the thumb and index finger of each hand, interlocking them (like two links of a chain).

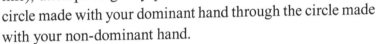

2. Hold light tension in both circles.

3. As you make a positive statement (e.g., your name or a food you like), attempt to gently pull the circle made with your dominant hand through the circle made with your non-dominant hand.

4. If the circle stays closed and interlocked, that is a "yes" response.

5. As you make a negative statement (e.g., a false name or saying you like a food you truly do not like), attempt to pull the circle made with your dominant hand through the circle made with your non-dominant hand.

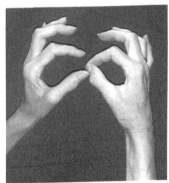

6. If the non-dominant circle allows the dominant hand circle to pull out, that is a "no" response.

ONE-HANDED TECHNIQUES

Finger Flick

1. Gently place tip of pinky fingernail onto fleshy part of thumb.

2. Make a positive statement and attempt to flick pinky from thumb.

3. The pinky will remain solid on the thumb with a "true" answer.

4. Now make a false statement and attempt to flick the pinky off the thumb.

5. The pinky fingernail will slide right off the thumb with a "false" answer.

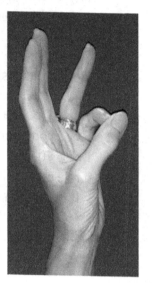

Finger Slide

1. The Finger Slide is similar to the Finger Flick.

2. Place the middle finger over the pointer fingernail.

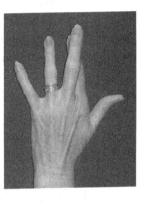

3. Make a positive statement and attempt to slide the top finger off the bottom fingernail.

4. The top finger will remain on the bottom finger with a "true" statement.

5. Make a false statement and attempt to slide the top finger off the bottom fingernail.

6. The top finger will slide right off the bottom fingernail with a "false" answer.

BONUS
MUSCLE TESTING ANOTHER PERSON

Note: Make sure the person has no shoulder issues before beginning because you don't want to potentially aggravate the problem.

1. Have the person stand facing you with one arm bent at a 90-degree angle. Tell the person to "hold firm," yet let the person know it is not a strength test. (Basically, you are doing the "Bent Arm" on another person.)

2. Place two fingers to the shoulder side of their wrist bone.

3. Ask them to "hold firm" when you gently press down.

4. The bent arm will be strong. You now have a baseline. There may be a slight give; however, it will still be noticeably strong.

5. Have the other person say "My name is _____." Gently press down on their arm while they hold firm. You should feel a solid "lock" in the muscle.

6. Have the other person say a false name with "My name is _____." Gently press down on their arm while they hold firm. There should be a weakness there, an inability for the muscle to "lock." Anything from a "bouncy" arm, one that wavers up and down because the muscle never locks, to an extreme weakness, where the arm just drops away, is considered weak.

Note: If you have difficulty telling a strong muscle from a weak muscle, it may be a sign of dehydration. After both of you take a sip or two of water, relax, take a deep breath, and begin again.

* * * * *

At the beginning of this book, I offered you a "heart-to-heart hug." Why heart-to-heart? Why not a regular hug?

Utilizing this bonus section about muscle testing others, follow these steps:

1. Verify their name.
2. Muscle test. Arm will be strong.
3. Have them say "fear, fear, fear."
4. Muscle test. Arm will be weak.
5. Have them say "love, love, love."
6. Muscle test. Arm will be strong.

You now have your baselines for strong and weak responses.

Next, give each other a regular hug. Muscle test the other person. Then, give each other a heart-to-heart hug. Muscle test the other person.

The muscle test response for the regular hug will be weak. The muscle test response for the heart-to-heart hug will be strong. Why is that?

It goes back to our being spiritual beings having a human experience. As spiritual beings, we are pure love and since we are also energy beings, and everything is energy, we are all connected. We communicate on a heartfelt level. The heart has its own strong energy field, extending many feet in all directions. In a heart-to-heart hug, this energy field interacts with the other person's heart energy field and energizes both of you. If you ask the other person to point to themselves, chances are they will point in the general direction of their heart and not their head.

So, why not connect with your fellow human beings and give them a heart-to-heart hug?

I leave you now...with a heart-to-heart hug - (H2HH). *Gratitude.*

Endnotes

Prelude

No notes.

Chapter 1 – Everything Is Energy

1   Additional information about the water studies can be found in *The Healing Power of Water, The Hidden Messages in Water,* and *Love Thyself* by Dr. Masaru Emoto.
2   Statistics for the percentage of water in the human body vary across study and researcher. One set of statistics is found on Page 147 of *The Energy Healing Experiments* by Gary E. Schwartz, PhD.
3   Quote is taken from Page 9 of *The Heartmath Solution* by Doc Childre and Howard Martin with Donna Beech.

Chapter 2 – Trapped Emotions

4   Quote is taken from Page 235 of *The Power of Infinite Love & Gratitude* by Dr. Darren R. Weissman.
5   Researchers and scientists debate the percentages of the conscious brain and the subconscious brain used during normal functioning. For the purposes of this book (and for the iceberg analogy), we will use the percentages discussed in the text of this chapter. Another such set of percentages is discussed in *The Emotion Code* by Dr. Bradley Nelson. See also www.DiscoverHealing.com.

Chapter 3 – Conventional Healing

6   The definition of conventional healing used here is the National Cancer Institute's definition found at https://www.cancer.gov/publications/dictionaries/cancer-terms?cdrid=449752.
7   An additional definition of conventional healing by Meredith Sackweitz, DO, can be found at https://www.sharecare.com/health/health-care-basics/what-is-conventional-medicine.

8   Additional information about the history of the pharmaceutical industry can be found at http://www4.dr-rath-foundation.org/THE_FOUNDATION/ history_of_the_pharma_cartel.html.

9   Quote is found at http://freedom-articles.toolsforfreedom.com/western-medicine-rockefeller-medicine/.

10 Quote is taken from Page xi of the "Preface" of *Your Body's Many Cries for Water* by F. Batmanghelidj, MD.

11 Information is found in https://en.wikipedia.org/wiki/Idiopathy.

Chapter 4 – Energy Healing

12 Quote can be found at *www.jungshim.org.uk/what-energy-healing*.

13 Quote is taken from "A Brief History of Energy Medicine" by Francesca McCartney, PhD, and can be found at *https://intuitionmedicine. org/a-brief-history-of-energy-medicine/*.

14 Additional information is available in *The Emotion Code* by Dr. Bradley Nelson, or from his website at www.DiscoverHealing.com.

15 Quote is taken from Page 147 of *The Energy Healing Experiments* by Gary E. Schwartz, PhD.

16 Researcher Albert Szent-Gyorgyi was the winner of the 1937 Nobel Prize in the category "Physiology or Medicine."

17 Quote is taken from the Access Consciousness® website www. accessconsciousness.com. Additional information about the modality and its creators can also be found at the site.

18 Additional information about The Body Code modality by Dr. Bradley Nelson, is available from his website at www.DiscoverHealing.com.

19 Additional information is available in *The Emotion Code* by Dr. Bradley Nelson, or from his website at www.DiscoverHealing.com.

20 Quote is taken from the website of *The LifeLine Technique*®, a modality developed by Dr. Darren R. Weissman: www.thelifelinecenter.com.

21 Additional information about The Reconnection can be found at www. thereconnection.com.

22 The term and its definition are taken from Page 2 of *The Everything Reiki Book* by Phylamenana lila Désy. Additional information about Reiki can be found at www.livescience.com/40275-reiki.html or www.reiki.org.

23 Additional information about Toning can be found at www.healingpath.info.

24 Additional information about Reiki can be found at www.livescience. com/40275-reiki.html and in *The Everything Reiki Book* by Phylamenana lila Désy.

25 Information about the types and sources of essential oils can be found on Page 3 of the *Essential Oils Desk Reference* published by Life Science Publishing.

26 Information about growing the plants from which to produce essential oils can be found on Page 17 of the *Essential Oils Integrative Medical Guide* by D. Gary Young.

27 Information about bacteria, viruses, and fungi and essential oils can be found on Page 11 of the *Essential Oils Desk Reference* published by Life Science Publishing.

Chapter 5 – Why Some May Say Emotional Release Healing May Not Work

28 Quote is taken from the "Master Extraordinary Success" page of the *Burgis Successful Solutions* website by Neal Burgis, PhD: https://www.successful-solutions.com/Pages/pain.html.

29 The example and definition of the concept of "drift" is found in "Well Adjusted," the December 20th entry of *A Deep Breath of Life* by Alan Cohen.

Chapter 6 – Barriers to Emotional Healing

30 Quote is taken from Page 18 of *You Can Heal Your Life* by Louise Hay.

Chapter 7 – How My Life Has Shifted…

31 Quote is taken from Page x of the "Preface" of *Your Body's Many Cries for Water* by F. Batmanghelidj, MD.

32 For more information about perception, read *The Power of Infinite Love & Gratitude* by Dr. Darren R. Weissman.

33 The story of the "tush cold" is found in "Stinkin' Thinkin'," the March 27th entry of *A Deep Breath of Life* by Alan Cohen.

Chapter 8 – Final Thoughts

34 Quote is taken from Page 10 of *Healing with the Angels* by Doreen Virtue.

Chapter 9 – Clients and Pets

No notes.

Chapter 10 – My Story

35 Additional information about Toning can be found at www.healingpath.info.

36 Quote is taken from Page 7 of *Knowledge of the Higher Worlds and Its Attainment* by Rudolf Steiner.

37 Additional information about the Theosophical Society can be found at the following website: www.*theosophicalsociety.org*.

38 To find out more about our perception of our environment, read especially page 89 of *The Biology of Belief* by Bruce H. Lipton, PhD.

Chapter 11 – Self-Muscle Testing

No notes.

Glossary

Akashic Records – Another term for the Akashic Records is an energetic "Book of Life." Each soul has its own set of books for each of its lifetimes. The Akashic Records contain every soul's history since Creation. They connect us to each other. Everything we want to know about ourselves is in the Akashic Records.

Attunement – During one's induction into the spiritual practice of Reiki, one gets attuned, or initiated, by having a Reiki Master share the knowledge of the Reiki energy. The ability to do Reiki can only be transferred from Master to student through Attunement, a process through which the student is "tuned" to a higher energy frequency. To learn more, check out the following two websites: www.radiantenergy.ca and www.reiki.org.

Awakened, Awakening – Also referred to as "spiritual awakening," "awakening" is a shift in consciousness or enlightenment that makes one more conscious of Universal truth (versus society's truths, which tend to be restrictive and oppressive). An "awakened" person has reconnected to self and to God/ Divine/Source.

Chronos Time – The Greeks have two words for time, *chronos* and *kairos*. Known as "man's time," *chronos* refers to time that can be measured, as in seconds, minutes, hours, days, and years. It is the root word for "chronological."

Dis-ease – The word "disease" is a medical term. This book is not about disease. Its purpose is, instead, to discuss physical or mental imbalances through the symptoms a person exhibits. These symptoms indicate a person is out-of-ease and, therefore, may suffer from dis-ease.

Download – When my thoughts or words are profound, or greater than what I, as me, would normally think or say, I call it a download from Above. It is God's way of talking to me through intuition.

Emotional Release – I use this term for the process of getting rid of emotional blockages.

Energetically – In physics, the term "energy" refers to the actual or potential power to move things. Those who follow metaphysical ways of thinking have co-opted this word to include one's vital energy or the tapping into the energy of the Universe.

Empath – One who can feel the emotions of another person, or even animals.

Healingness – This is a word I made up to mean the act of being healed.

Ho'oponopono Prayer – This prayer is an ancient powerful Hawaiian prayer for reconciliation and forgiveness. A Hawaiian therapist, Dr. Ihaleakala Hew Len states that since we are all connected, we are responsible for each other – and that means anyone in our life, no matter what the connection, close friend or mere acquaintance, even Mother Earth. Therefore, when we pray this prayer, we look within and ask for forgiveness and ultimately love ourselves, thus healing us and those around us. To begin, we identify and state who or what we are praying for. The prayer goes like this and is repeated several times:

> *Mother Earth* (for example),
> *I love you.*
> *I am sorry.*
> *Please forgive me.*
> *Thank you.*

Kairos Time – *Kairos* is God's time, Universal time. It is a Greek word meaning the right or opportune time. Thus, everything has its own time. There is a season for everything. We cannot alter *kairos*, no matter how hard we try.

Kool – This is my slang term to express a feeling or attitude. I use it instead of the word "cool," which normally applies to temperature.

Law of Attraction – When one focuses on positive or negative thoughts, one can bring positive or negative experiences into one's life. The Law of Attraction involves all aspects of life: thoughts, words, circumstances, people, and ideas. Everything is energy; thus, everyone, everything, is connected in one way or another.

Law of Free Will – The Law of Free Will is a universal law, a cosmic law. One has the *choice* to decide how to respond to any situation, to act on one's own convictions.

Meridians – Meridians are highways of life energy within the body. There are twelve meridians in lateral and symmetrical distribution throughout the body. They exist as corresponding pairs. There are 365 acupuncture points, with each belonging to particular meridians, which in turn are connected to specific organs.

Metaphysical – The base word of metaphysics comes from two Greek base words: "meta," meaning over and beyond, and "physics," meaning the science of energy, matter, motion, and force. There are a few definitions of metaphysical. I use the term to describe a spiritual philosophy or way of life, the search for Universal truth, the meaning of life, the relationship of man, mind, and God/Universe.

Miasm – The word "miasm" has its roots in the Greek language, translating as "fault" or "taint," and was first coined by Hippocrates. It is any inherited physical or mental tendency that can occur through multiple generations. To learn more, check out both of the following websites: www.wholehealthnow.com/homeopathy pro/miasms and www.homeopathyhome.com.

Negative Energy – I apply this term to anyone who is a downer, sees only the negative in life, loves emotional drama and negativity, is judgmental, and complains. I also apply it to any thoughts, words, actions, movies, or music that are negative in nature.

Neophyte – This term refers to anyone who is new to a skill or subject matter, even a belief.

Nutritionals – This is a term I use to include all vitamins and supplements, anything to nourish the body other than food.

Positive Energy – I apply this term to anyone who is uplifting; who exhibits faith, has gratitude and thus sees the positive in all things, even in a not-so-positive situation; who makes a choice to be happy; and who helps others for the sake of helping rather than for how it affects their ego and public persona. I also apply it to any thoughts, words, actions, movies, or music that are positive in nature.

Subconscious Reactionary Pattern – The subconscious mind operates under the survival mechanism of fight or flight. It operates the automatic (done out of habit) and the autonomic (involuntary) systems of our body. When a trapped emotion is activated, or triggered, in any manner, behavioral or physical symptoms occur as a subconscious response, usually as a pattern of reaction – hence the term subconscious reactionary pattern.

Synchronicity – This word is similar to "coincidence." However, "coincidence" applies to two or more events happening simultaneously, whereas, "synchronicity" implies a higher intelligence at work and is thus more related to energetic connections.

Unawakened – I use this term for anyone who has yet to realize that we are all energy beings having a human experience. In this state of consciousness, spirituality is still stuck in intellectualism. An "unawakened" person may not yet fully appreciate the power of gratitude.

Web of Belief – The term, *web of belief,* was coined by a 20th Century philosopher, Willard Van Orman Quine. Each of us functions within our own personal set of beliefs, and those beliefs are mutually reinforcing knowledge claims about the way the world works. We may change some of our beliefs as we go along in life, yet the core of our web is made up of those deep-seated beliefs and is difficult to change or eliminate.

Helpful Quotes

Forgiveness is the only sane response. ~ A Course in Miracles

The only response to your brother is gratitude. ~ A Course in Miracles

Circumstances do not make the man – they reveal him. ~ James Allen

Two men looked out through prison bars; one saw mud, the other, stars. ~ James Allen

Holding resentment is like eating poison and then waiting for the other person to keel over. ~ Anonymous

If I keep busy, I won't have to look at what is frightening me. ~ Anonymous

Never underestimate the power of a kind act. ~ Anonymous

The darkest hour is just before the dawn. ~ Anonymous

Never utter these words: "I do not know this, therefore it is false." One must study to know; know to understand; understand to judge. ~ Apothegm of Narada

I imagine that one of the reasons people cling to their hate so stubbornly is because they sense, once hate is gone, they will be forced to deal with pain. ~ James Baldwin, *Notes of a Native Son*

Joy is the most ineffable sign of the presence of God. ~ Leon Bloy

The pessimist sees difficulty in every opportunity. The optimist sees the opportunity in every difficulty. ~ Winston Churchill

It is hard to defeat an enemy who has an outpost in your own head. ~ Sally Compton

Only by self-respect will you compel others to respect you. ~ Fydor Dostoevsky

Our lives are a sum total of the choices we have made. ~ Wayne Dyer

Do the thing you fear, and the death of fear is certain. ~ Ralph Waldo Emerson

What lies behind you and what lies in front of you, pales in comparison to what lies inside of you. ~ Ralph Waldo Emerson

If someone in your life talked to you the way you talk to yourself, you would have left them long ago. ~ Dr. Carla Gordan

Train your mind to see the good in every situation. ~ Kushandwizdom

It's a funny thing about life; if you accept anything but the very best, you will get it. ~ Somerset Maugham

Be kind. Everyone you meet is carrying a heavy burden. ~ Ian MacLaren, *Beside the Bonnie Brier*

One small positive thought in the morning can change your whole entire day. ~ www.Positivelifetips.com

If your everyday life seems poor, don't blame it; blame yourself; admit to yourself that you are not enough of a poet to call forth its riches. ~ Rainer Maria Rilke

All truths pass through three stages. First, it is ridiculed. Second, it is violently opposed. Third, it is accepted as being self-evident. ~ Arthur Schopenhauer, German philosopher (1788-1860)

The most difficult part of bringing medical care to the natives was getting them to give up their superstitions. ~ Dr. Albert Schweitzer

Every human being is the author of his own health or disease... ~Swami Sivananda (1887-1963)

If you want something you've never had, you must be willing to do something you've never done. ~ Unknown, as seen in a café window

...nothing is ever as bleak as it looks. Everything, in fact, is a blessing... How can a sudden, calamitous event in one's life be a blessing? It takes a longer view...all calamities are blessings, not yet understood by the Mind. ~ Neale Donald Walsh
(See full quote at today@nealedonaldwalsch.com, 3 March 2017.)

Life begins at the end of your comfort zone. ~ Neale Donald Walsh

We turn to God for help when our foundation is shaking, only to recognize that it is God who is shaking it. ~ Charles Weston

Our deepest fear is not that we are inadequate. Our deepest fear is that we are powerful beyond measure. It is our light, not our darkness that most frightens us. ~ Marianne Williamson

Do...or do not. There is no try. ~ Yoda, in "The Empire Strikes Back"

Many of the truths we cling to depend on our point of view. ~ Yoda

Recommended Readings

Awakening to the Secret Code of Your Mind, Your Mind's Journey to Inner Peace by Dr. Darren R. Weissman

Celestine Prophecy by James Redfield

Final Gifts: Understanding the Special Awareness, Needs, and Communications of the Dying by Maggie Callanan and Patricia Kelley

The Biology of Belief by Bruce H. Lipton, PhD

The Emotion Code by Dr. Bradley Nelson

The Energy Bus by Jon Gordon

The Energy Healing Experiments by Gary E. Schwartz, PhD

Feelings Buried Alive Never Die by Karol K. Truman

The Healing Power of Water by Masaru Emoto

The Heartmath Solution by Doc Childre and Howard Martin with Donna Beech

The Hidden Messages in Water by Masaru Emoto

The Invisible Force by Dr. Wayne W. Dyer

Journey of Souls by Michael Newton

Joyfully Shattered by Rick Sheff, MD

Knowledge of the Higher Worlds and Its Attainment by Rudolf Steiner

Love Thyself by Masaru Emoto

Orthomolecular Medicine for Everyone by Abram Hoffer, MD, PhD and Andrew W. Saul, PhD

Out on a Limb by Shirley MacLaine

The Power of Infinite Love & Gratitude by Dr. Darren R. Weissman

The Reconnection by Dr. Eric Pearl

The Secret by Rhonda Byrnes

The Wisdom of Emotions by Dr. David F. Coppola

You Can Heal Your Life by Louise L. Hay

Your Body's Many Cries for Water by F. Batmanghelidj

About the Author

Susan Olencki Giangiulio is a wellness advocate and a practicing energy healer, specializing in emotional release healing since 2009. She is a certified practitioner in The Emotion Code, the LifeLine Technique®, and other healing modalities. She also integrates essential oils into her practice.

Susan took a circuitous route to becoming the wellness advocate she is today. She began her career as an international fashion model and segued into managing a garment showroom in New York City. Later, she held various positions at network and affiliate television stations. Due to lifelong scoliosis, she began, in earnest, her current journey: delving into the various holistic approaches to healing the body.

Susan was born and raised in Ann Arbor, Michigan. After graduating from the University of Michigan, where she earned a Bachelor of Arts degree in Education, she lived and worked in New York City, London, Barcelona, Zurich, San Francisco, Monterey, Sacramento, and Naples, Italy. Prior to getting married, she earned her Master's in Education. She currently resides in Florida where she owns a wellness business, Back to Basic Wellness (www.b2bw.us), with her husband Tony, a retired Air Force officer.

Printed in the United States
By Bookmasters